The
POWER
of
NEURO-
PLASTICITY

SHAD HELMSTETTER, PH.D.

The Power of Neuroplasticity

Published by Park Avenue Press
362 Gulf Breeze Pkwy., #104
Gulf Breeze, FL 32561

Helmstetter, Shad
The Power of Neuroplasticity

ISBN-10: 1499794606
ISBN-13: 978-1499794601

For information on
listening to self-talk audio programs:
www.SelfTalkPlus.com

Other books by Shad Helmstetter, Ph.D.

What to Say When You Talk to Your Self
365 Days of Positive Self-Talk
365 Days of Positive Self-Talk for Finding Your Purpose
365 Days of Positive Self-Talk for Weight-Loss
The Incredible Adventures of Shadrack the
Self-Talk Bear (Children's books)
The Boy Who Wanted to Change the World (Autobiography)

Table of Contents

Chapter 1

Neuroplasticity—Big Word, Beautiful Meaning

"You are creating, at this moment, the person you're going to become tomorrow, and you are physically wiring that person into your brain."

This is a book about giving people freedom, and giving people hope.

For many years, we believed that the human brain stopped growing or changing when we were young—and everything we were taught about our behavior was based on that belief. We now know differently.

The breakthrough of the discovery of neuroplasticity is that *your brain is designed to change throughout your lifetime.* Your brain is changing at this moment. Right now, no matter where you are in your life or what age you are, while you're reading this, your brain is literally rewiring itself.

From the latest research and from the use of new technology that allows us for the first time to look deeply into the human brain *while it's working,* we have begun to learn

11

more about how the brain is wired and how it works. And most importantly, we have learned the role that our *thoughts* play in the wiring of the brain and the creation of our success as individuals.

Keeping it Simple and Making it Work

In the following pages, you'll find information and ideas that will help you reintroduce yourself to your own mind in some amazing ways. Although this book includes information that originated from research in the field of neuroscience, this isn't a textbook with scientific jargon that requires a background in neuroscience to understand it. I've done my best to bring a great deal of information together, sort it all out, condense it, and put it in words anyone can understand.

You'll find the tone of this book to be positive and uplifting. In writing it, I've applied the same principles we'll be talking about throughout the book—principles such as *intention, focus,* and *repetition.*

You'll also notice there's a deliberate balance between information and action steps you can put into practice right away. The suggestions and ideas I recommend to you are practical and down to earth, and you should be able to use and apply them even before you finish reading.

Whether you find just one new gem of an idea here, or a dozen new thoughts or ideas that apply to you, rest assured that by the time you read the final chapter, you will understand what your own mind and brain can do for you, and what you can do to make those positive changes happen.

As you read, I encourage you to open your mind, let the new ideas flow in easily and let them sink in. Read the book with your determined *intention* to gain every ounce of new knowledge and awareness you can possibly glean from the ideas presented here.

There's a reason to do this. We have learned that *your conscious intention to do something increases your brain's ability to wire in new ideas!* It is my hope that with your conscious intention to learn the ideas expressed here, they will make a positive and valuable contribution to how you think, the actions you take, and the results you achieve.

Helping Your Brain's Neuroplasticity Work for You

The discovery of neuroplasticity did not begin with what it can do for the mind. The initial discovery started by helping stroke victims regain the use of muscles they once thought useless, and teaching people with learning and physical disabilities how to literally rewire and retrain their brain functions.

But it is what lies beyond the world of medical research, moving into the world of mind research, which promises to affect the lives of even more of us in truly incredible ways. It is how we can personally use the discovery of neuroplasticity in our everyday lives—*and learn to rewire our brains for ourselves*—that is making a critical difference for countless individuals.

It was research in the field of neuroscience that first alerted researchers in other fields such as medicine, education, training, and counseling to the properties of what

13

the brain's neuroplasticity offers us. In this book, we will focus on the aspects of neuroplasticity that deal with improving brain potential and function, such as:

Personal growth
Reaching your goals
Mindfulness
Intention
The importance of belief
Creating a positive attitude
Changing your self-talk
Overcoming negativity
Mental sharpness and clarity
Meditation
Increasing your level of happiness
Improving your brain's acuity
Staying younger, longer

Not only have we learned what the most essential tools of brain enhancement and personal growth really are, we have also finally learned how positive, personal change actually takes place in the brain, and how to use that amazing neurological process to make our lives better.

What we've learned is changing our world.

What goes on in your mind and in your life—changes your brain, *physically*. When you think or do something repeatedly, your brain actually changes its physical structure. Your environment, your experiences, your emotions, your attitudes, your self-talk, all of your perceptions—your brain is imprinting itself with every message it gets. And this discovery means that because your brain is constantly rewiring and changing itself, *you are creating, at this moment, the person you're going to become tomorrow, and you are physically wiring that person into your brain.* That is the remarkable power of neuroplasticity at work.

What is the Future You Will Write Today?

Your brain's neuroplasticity works both in grand ways and in small ways. Some people who put this power to work in their own lives will change things like an attitude that's negative, a career that isn't working, finances that don't add up, or a relationship that isn't going as well as it should.

Many readers will use this book to enhance or change their career path, turn the dream of a new home into a reality, or reach high-level goals like traveling the world, creating a legacy of long-term wealth, or helping the less fortunate.

Still others will read this book to learn to use the increased power of their brain to become sharper, have a better memory, get smarter and more in control, and stay younger longer.

We all have our dreams and our goals. Wherever you are in your life right now, and whatever positive goal you have in front of you, you get to direct it. *You get to literally wire your brain to take you there.*

With the discovery of neuroplasticity in the human brain, our old notion that our lives are set, that we are destined by our genes and our past to follow the path that fortune gave us, has been thrown out the window.

With what we have learned, your *past* isn't what counts. Because your brain is constantly rewiring itself with the

15

repeated new messages it receives, how you decide to wire your brain *next* is what counts.

One of my favorite Bible passages is Romans 12:2, which says, *". . . be transformed by the renewing of your mind."* That's a powerful exhortation, and I couldn't agree with it more. As we will see, your brain's ability to be transformed, literally happens in very practical and life-changing ways—as a result of the renewing of your mind.

This book is about the renewed mind. It will show you that it's not *where you've been*, it's where you choose to go *next*, that counts. It's not who you've *been;* it's who you decide to *become*—and that changes the story you're about to live.

A Personal Story about Rewiring the Brain

When I decided some years ago to write my first book, *"What to Say When You Talk to Your Self,"* about how our self-talk changes our lives, the people I knew at that time could be divided into two groups: those who thought I would write the book, and those who doubted it, or thought it was a foolish or impossible idea. The ones who spoke against the idea of writing the book thought it would fail. Those who thought I would do it decided to believe in my goal, and waited to see what would happen.

I made the choice to try something new—a way to rewire my brain with the belief that I *could* do it—and not accept any mental wiring that said that I could *not*. What I decided to do was to leave any disbeliefs or doubters behind, and approach the goal in a different way.

The Power of Neuroplasticity

On Thursday, October 3rd, 1985, I got on an airplane and flew to Corpus Christi, Texas. There, I rented a car and drove to a ferry that took me to the small gulf-side town of Port Aransas on Mustang Island off the coast of Texas, where I rented a condo unit overlooking the Gulf. While I was there, in complete isolation, I wrote my book.

But I didn't just go to the island and immediately start writing. For two weeks after I arrived, before I wrote a single word of the book, I did nothing but walk on the beach by myself, look at the waves, watch the seagulls, and talk to myself about the book I was going to write.

Instead of listening to the doubts of others or any doubts from my past, I decided to bring a goal to life. The goal was that the book I had come there to write would still be on the shelves of bookstores, not a year or two later, but *twenty* years later. A tall order! At the time, most self-help books would be popular for a year or so, and then usually fade out of sight. My goal meant the book I was going to write would go twenty years better than that.

After walking on the beach, watching the waves, talking to myself and using a lot of positive self-talk for two long weeks, I went back to the condo unit I had rented, sat down at my computer, looked out over the water, and began to write. The first words I wrote were:

"You are everything that is. Your thoughts, your life, your dreams come true. You are everything you choose to be. You are as unlimited as the endless universe."

For the next three months, along with continuing to walk on the beach each day, talking to myself, and listening to self-

17

talk, I wrote every day. My schedule was: write, go to bed, sleep, get up, write, go to bed, sleep, get up, and keep writing.

I don't remember a day during that intense writing time that I looked back at the doubts or the doubters. I just focused forward, kept talking to myself in the most positive possible way, and kept writing.

Because of my long walks on the beach each day for two weeks before I began to write, instead of being guided by doubt, I was guided by my goal—to write a book that would help people get better, all over the world, and to deliver a message that would be just as relevant twenty years later, as it was when it was written. (My reasoning was that if I was determined to write a lasting book, each sentence and paragraph I wrote would be written more clearly and more meaningfully.)

Three months after I had arrived on the island, I packed up my computer, paid my rent, took the ferry back to the mainland, turned in my rental car at the airport, and flew home with my completed manuscript in hand. A few months later, my book had been edited, and the final draft went to press. Not long after that, the book was in full release nationwide, and I was appearing on television programs like Oprah Winfrey and CNN.

The book did what it was supposed to do. I reached my twenty-year goal a few years ago, and that book remains on the self-help best-seller lists nearly thirty years after it was written. In fact, I recently worked on *"What to Say When You Talk to Your Self"* again, when I updated the book for its publication in e-book editions.

During the writing of the book you're reading now, I received a box of books in the mail. They were from a publisher in India, who sent me newly published editions of *"What to Say When You Talk to Your Self,"* printed in Telugu, Tamil, and Hindi. The book some people thought I would never write is now published in over seventy countries.

I'm not applauding myself for the life that book has lived. I did nothing more than set a goal and choose to see it through. I simply refused to listen to the impossibilities of my past and the doubts of others, and chose instead to do something others told me could not be done.

The important point to the story is this: day after day, walking on that beach, looking at the sky and the seagulls and the sandpipers and the waves along the shore, I was *thinking* with clarity, focus, and intention about what I would do, and the steps I would take to make my dream become a reality. By so doing, I literally wired my brain to help me accomplish my goal. The steps that made it work *were the steps I was taking in the sand.*

When I was walking on the beach and talking to myself each day, *I was rewiring my brain.*

Chapter 2

The Holy Grail of Personal Growth

The secret to the true source of personal growth has been sought through the ages, and this quest has continued to the present day. Mystics, spiritual leaders, philosophers, and today's motivational trainers have all searched for the true path to personal success. *What is the secret to each man or woman's destiny? Why do some people fail, while others succeed?* With the answers to those questions, the future of mankind is much brighter and more hopeful than it was just a few years ago.

Many people have looked for the answer in the field of self-improvement. For more than 50 years, a generation of self-help authors taught us what they were discovering about how each of us could improve our lives. And they told us we would find the best in our lives when we learned and practiced the "rules" of personal growth they had discovered.

The rules they gave us were not difficult to understand. And, not surprisingly, most of the popular self-help authors, in one way or another, identified many of the same rules. If you read the greatest self-help books of the past decades, you'll recognize the rules they taught us: *set goals; think positive; learn to be organized; manage your time; remember that you create what you believe in most; focus on what you want to achieve; work hard, and never give up.*

(In these pages, we'll meet some of these ideas again, but we'll be looking at them in a new, updated and more scientific light. As we've now discovered, the key to each of them working is neuroplasticity.)

Success is in the Brain

When I wrote the book *"What to Say When You Talk to Your Self,"* I had studied self-help concepts that were working in many lives. Because the ideas were working, and were literally changing lives, it became clear to me that *these concepts must have their basis in the physical, neural anatomy of the brain itself.*

The science behind the development of personal growth was not yet fully understood, of course. However, it was undeniable that personal improvement methods like changing one's attitude, thinking positively, and setting goals, were working.

I wanted to know *why* they were working. I believed that the rules of personal growth, while sound, should be taken to the next step into how the *brain itself* works—physically, chemically, electrically—neurologically. Lasting success had to be a product of the mind, but also a product of how the brain is *wired.*

That book presented my findings that personal growth in any *repeatable* form is never an *accident*; that success is the result

21

of mental *programs* that begin at birth, and often stay with us throughout our lives. The book identified the importance of *self-talk* as a practical way to change those programs, based on the premise that *your brain is changed by the thoughts you think.*

Interestingly, during the time that many thousands of people were applying the principles of personal growth and clearly improving their lives as a result, "self-help" also had its doubters. These were well-intentioned critics who questioned the promises of positive attitude and other forms of self-help, saying that things like *positive* thinking were nothing more than *wishful* thinking, and that there was nothing scientific about them. As surprising as it seems now, some of that skepticism came from the field of neuroscience.

While Dr. Norman Vincent Peale, Napoleon Hill, and Dr. Maxwell Maltz, three of the most popular proponents of personal growth of the 20th century, were saying that your attitude and your thinking could change your life from the inside out, neuroscientists were still saying that positive thinking was like any other kind of thinking, and that it could not actually *change* the human brain. Those neuroscientists were defending the long-held scientific paradigm that the brain stops growing or changing early in life, and as a result, you could not actually "change" your brain no matter what you thought.

It was clear that many neuroscientists were continuing to defend a picture of the brain that was out of line with what we were observing in our studies of human behavior.

My own study and findings disagreed with views that I believed to be outdated. I recognized that many people, whether they were very young or were in their 80s or older, were making dramatic and often *permanent* changes in their lives, and they were clearly making those changes by changing the way they *thought*.

So I continued to research and write several more books on the subject, and continued to present my position that the human brain could be *rewired* and *changed* by what we thought—the input we gave it. This concept was so important, in fact, that some years later, I founded the Life Coach Institute to help others, as life coaches, teach and apply this guiding principle.

In time, what we at the Institute knew to be true about the brain's ability to change would become universally accepted fact. But in the meanwhile, schools and universities continued to teach that the brain is set, and stops growing and changing before we reach adulthood. According to the textbooks from that time, each of us had to live with the brain we ended up with for the rest of our lives. We were taught that our genes determine who we are and who we become, and that the brain cannot grow or change. We were told that with aging, the brain inevitably loses its vitality and suppleness, and in time, even its memories.

And that was that! For years, that's what we were told, that's what all textbooks taught, and that's what most people believed.

Fortunately for us today, what our textbooks were teaching us then, was wrong.

A New Picture of Who We Are

Finally, after many years of thinking the old way about the brain, within the space of a few short years, a new era of computer-imagining technology stepped in. New experiments could be conducted that proved the *right* kind of self-help thinking had been on the right track all along. With the new technology, scientists were able to see a very *different* picture of the human brain. And neuroscience began to change *its* mind.

For the first time, with new research technology such as Positron Emission Tomography (PET), Functional Magnetic Resonance Imaging (fMRI), Transcranial Magnetic Stimulation (TMS), and other new tools for brain imaging and mapping, neuroscientists were able to "see inside" the brain, *while it was working*. And what they saw, literally changed their overall picture of the way the brain actually works.

For the first time, scientists saw that the human brain, instead of being set and static, continually reprogrammed and restructured itself. They saw that the brain grew and changed, moment by moment, input by input, and thought by thought. The brain was *plastic*, malleable, and it was not only growing new neurons, it was *rewiring* itself! And this amazing plasticity wasn't only happening in the brains of the young; *it was happening throughout the entire lifetime of each individual!*

With the discovery that the brain is continually rewiring itself based on new input it receives, we had finally found the scientific "holy grail" of personal growth. It is that the brain itself is plastic, and able to change, and that plasticity creates a *neural activity feedback loop*. That is, the brain sets up a continuing, self-perpetuating cycle of success or failure that lies at the heart of why we act, live, and feel as we do.

It is the one scientific discovery that stands above all others in the field of personal growth—and it explains why the truth about neuroplasticity itself is so important.

Finding the Grail

The "holy grail" of personal growth has been an elusive goal for so many people who wanted to make their lives better. Now, with the discovery that the brain rewires itself with the input we give it, we have found the answer we were looking for: if you want to change your life, change your wiring.

The latest research from the field of neuroscience is incredibly promising. You get to go past the problems or the self-imagined inadequacies of your past, and create the better, more amazing person you would like to be. And you don't have to hope for a miracle, or wait for luck to happen. This time, science is on your side. We have found the holy grail of personal growth: *You can rewire your brain.*

Chapter 3

How it Works

The process of rewiring your brain in your favor is a complex process in the brain itself, but as we've learned more about how it works, we've become more able to understand it and simplify it.

Your brain grows and changes based on feedback. What you tell it, changes it. And while it's rewiring itself, your brain then feeds those new programs, those new pictures of yourself, back to you. It's a feedback "loop." What you put in, you get back out, in a continuous *"neural activity feedback loop."*

Even for readers who are not accustomed to the terminology, this is easy to understand. The neural activity feedback loop just means you're talking to your brain, and your brain is changing based on what you tell it. And your brain responds by giving you an update on how it's doing. It's growing and changing, and it lets you see those changes in the way you think and how you feel.

By the time you've read this one chapter, you'll have a good understanding of that feedback loop, and why it's so important to you.

Creating a Self-Fulfilling Prophecy

The neural activity feedback loop is the process by which:

Everything we think, feel, or do, imprints or rewires our brain. Our rewired brain, in turn, affects everything we think, feel, or do . . . which again, in turn, imprints or rewires our brain.

Our perceptions wire our brain, and our brain, in turn, affects our perceptions. It is an endless loop that begins before we're born and continues to the moment of our last breath.

Here's an example of how the neural activity feedback loop works in one person's everyday life.

Let's say that when Mark gets up in the morning, he hasn't slept well, and he has the feeling it's going to be *"one of those days"*—not a good sign. Mark gets dressed, has breakfast, and anxiously gets ready for the day. He's been worried about how well he's going to do with the presentation he has to make at work today, and he feels he'll be lucky if he gets through it without a stumble. He's afraid he's going to mess it up. As he drives to work, he doesn't notice his fingers endlessly drumming on the steering wheel, another sign that he's far from being at his best. When he greets his boss, Mark's smile is painted in place, but underneath he's doing anything but smiling.

In spite of his reservations, Mark has to make the presentation, so he does. As he expected, it doesn't go well, and he's not surprised. He's never felt he was very good in front of a group. At the end of the day, Mark goes home and, after an evening of feeling dejected and watching television, he goes to bed. He does his best to forget the day—it wasn't his first day like this. Maybe tomorrow will be better. *"Probably not"* is the last thing he hears his mind say to him as he finally drifts off to sleep and leaves the day to the past.

Was it the Day, or was it His Programs?

Here's what actually happened: Mark didn't get up on the wrong side of the bed; he got up on the wrong side of his *programs*.

Every message Mark gave his brain was that it was going to be a bad day, that he was going to do a terrible job giving the presentation, and that nothing would work out right. Most of us know the dangers of a negative pep talk. But chemically, in Mark's brain, there was more going on than just a few momentary misgivings.

With each questioning thought, Mark was sending messages to his brain that called up *other* negative programs of self-doubt that he'd already programmed in and stored up in the past. So he *started* the day with the message to his brain that said, *"Make me fail. That's what I've done before. That's what I expect to do today."*

That, of course, turned out to be a self-fulfilling prophecy. But here's why: Mark's brain, using its neural activity feedback loop, recorded his mood and his lack of confidence. Then his brain immediately began to search for other, previously stored neural networks that *agreed* with his self-doubt—and in this case, there were a ton of them.

When his brain pulled all those other, equally negative programs together, chemically and electrically in his brain, they voted. The vote was taken, and in seconds, the results were in. Mark was right. *He was going to have a bad day.*

In this case, Mark fed negative, doubting messages to his brain; his brain recorded those messages, and then fed them back to him, along with a whole lot of other negative programs of the same kind. That's the feedback loop.

It was not even how stressed Mark was, or how tired he was, that caused him to fail. It was not fate or luck. And it wasn't the day. It was a series of neural, chemical, electrical connections in Mark's brain that brought up failing programs from his past, that he called upon to help him fail—and they did.

Mark did not know he was doing this, of course— directing his own failure. It was almost entirely unconscious. *All Mark had to do was set it up*, and his brain, with its years of negative programs stored up for an occasion just like this, took it from there.

For each of us, our neural activity feedback loop does all that because it's designed to get input, record it, store it, and with enough repetition, wire in a new neural pathway—and finally, *act on that pathway as though it were true.*

Had Mark set up the day differently, in advance, it might have worked out differently. Better instructions to his brain would have set up his day in an entirely different way. His brain would have called up better, more positive programs from his past. That same brain that helped him fail could have helped Mark create an attitude of belief, inspiration, and optimism—instead of the opposite—and it very likely would have created different results.

Because of his brain's neural activity feedback loop, Mark simply got back out of his brain what he had put *into* it—and what he had told it to do. In so doing, Mark's brain duly recorded one more failure, and quietly and competently strengthened the *pathway of failure*, cementing it even more firmly into place in his brain.

A Lifetime of Programs

We can learn a lot from seeing even a small picture of a single day in Mark's life. It lets us see how this feedback loop works in even the smallest details of life. But it is the larger, macro view of the neural activity feedback loop which gives us a greater insight.

Instead of dealing with just a single day, that loop deals with *every* day of our lives, and will continue to do so for each of us from here on out. What this feedback loop does, will affect virtually everything about us.

No matter what it is, *when you think it, your brain records it.* In that same moment, your brain *compares that thought* to every other neural program it has previously stored that agrees with it.

In that moment, your brain not only acts on those programs, but it also begins to record the same messages again, making them stronger.

In time, your brain will continue to rerecord programs, making them so strong that you can actually believe they are "real," part of who you are. And thought by thought, moment by moment, day by day, you act out the results.

Happy Brain . . . *Unhappy* Brain

A friend of mine was visiting a doctor who was working in her lab, studying brain samples of people who were deceased.

The doctor would examine a sample of a brain under a microscope and say, "*Un*happy brain." Then she would examine another sample and say "*Happy* brain." Studying a number of brain samples, commenting on each of them in turn, she said, "*Un*happy brain ... *happy* brain ... *unhappy* brain ..." and so on.

My friend was very curious about what she was doing, and asked the doctor what it meant.

"You can see a microcosm of their lives in these tissue samples of their brains," she said. "Some brains lived an unhappy life. Other brains look *healthy*. I call them h*appy* brains. You can almost tell, from looking at their brains, which people lived happy lives and which people didn't."

When people hear that story, the first question that comes to mind is what their own brains look like. It makes you wonder how your own brain would fare. There's a way to get an idea of what your brain might look like, while there's still a chance to do something about it.

What Color is Your Brain?

You may already suspect what you'd find. But if you could actually see what the woman in the lab saw by looking at a picture of your own brain, you'd want to know for sure whether your brain was a "happy brain" or an "unhappy brain." There's a way you can do that, without having to wait for a lab technician to examine a sample of your brain after you've passed on.

Here's how to do it. Artists who create illustrations of the brain often use different colors to denote different areas of brain function. In this case, I'd like you to "color your brain" in a different way.

Let's say you have a picture of your brain, a simple outline sketch with nothing colored in. Now let's say you have three colored pens. One is *gold*, one is *gray*, and one is *neutral*, with no color. What we'll do in this illustration is to color your brain with the *thoughts* you think.

The gold pen is for your most clearly positive, healthy thoughts. The gray pen is for your negative thoughts. And the neutral pen without color is for thoughts that are neither one nor the other.

In our illustration, we're not coloring in one or another area of the brain to show the sections of the brain and what each of them does. We're coloring in the entire brain, to show us the *quality* of our *thoughts*.

Let's start by coloring your "brain picture" for just one day. I'll ask you to imagine keeping your brain picture with you for the entire day. As we begin, to give you an example of how it works, I'll start by asking you the question, *"How are you today?"* (You can answer that, now, in your mind.)

If your answer was *"Fine,"* or *"Okay,"* imagine you take the "neutral" colored pen, and make a neutral mark somewhere on your brain picture. If you said, *"Incredible,"* or *"Outstanding,"* mentally use the gold pen and make one gold mark anywhere on the picture. If you said, *"My day is terrible,"* or *"Who cares?"* visualize selecting the gray pen and making one gray-colored mark on your picture.

As you go through just this one day, every time you think a conscious thought that you're aware of, stop for a moment, mentally select the pen that most accurately describes your thought—positive, negative, or neutral—and make a mark on your brain picture. Do the same thing for the entire day. Everything you say, everything you think, take a moment, decide what color it should be, and mark your picture.

There are different views on how many thoughts each of us thinks in a day; estimates range from 12,500 to 70,000 or more. For purposes of coloring in our brain picture, we'll use the number 35,000 as the number of individual thoughts each of us has in a day. That would mean you'd have to make 35,000 colored marks on your brain picture in one day. (Big job!)

At the end of the first day, how would your picture look? If you had actually colored in everything you said, and every thought you thought, either *gold, neutral,* or *gray*—positive, neutral, or negative—*what color would your brain picture show the most?*

Imagine doing that for a month. Then imagine doing it for a year. At the end of a year, if you had marked in a color that represented everything you said and every thought you thought, what color would your brain picture be?

The purpose of this exercise is to let you know that although you may not be carrying colored pens with you and coloring in each thought you think, your brain is doing exactly that. Coloring your brain is the essence of the neural activity feedback loop. Your brain is, right now, looking at the color of your thoughts, recording them, programming them in, and sending those colors back to you as a picture of you.

Think of anyone you know, and ask yourself, "Is that person a *"gold,"* *"neutral,"* or *"gray?"* Whatever color they have, remember that their own words and thoughts—their programs—are giving them their colors.

A Lifetime of Coloring Your Brain

Now, instead of looking at your brain picture to see what color it is after coloring it in for just one day, or even for a year, let's look at that same picture of your brain over your entire lifetime. When you look at your own brain picture now, fully colored in with every thought you've ever thought, *what is the predominant color of your brain?* What color is it *most?*

If it's filled with gold, that's good. That's also unusual. Most people have a lot of negative, gray marks that came from gray experiences and self-doubts that were recorded by their brains, as though that's who they are. (That's not who they have to be; that's just what their brains have recorded in the past.)

Your brain is designed to feed back to you, and reproduce, the "colors"—the *attitudes,* the *opinions,* and the *beliefs* about life and about yourself—you have that are the strongest. That's why people who have the most positive disposition create more of the same, and why people who are down and negative continue to act and think in a negative way. Life around us can change, but each day we view life through the *color* that dominates the picture of our brain.

In our earlier example, *what was the color of Mark's brain?* In the short picture we saw, Mark had created a brain that was not colored gold. It was colored gray, and bordering on dark gray.

As you can easily imagine, a different Mark—one who looked at things differently, one who had a brain with more gold in it, more positive programs—might have used his brain's feedback loop completely differently.

This better, wiser Mark, knowing he had an important presentation to make at work the next day, would properly prepare himself the night before for his presentation, and also reassure himself of his most positive possibilities for the next day. He wouldn't be lying to himself, or kidding himself; he would be presenting his brain *with the best messages of success* he had stored up in his past.

In the morning, in the first moments of awareness, *this* Mark would fill his mind with the uplifting emotions of positive potential, and he would restate the self-talk that says, *"I can do this. Now is my time. Today is my day. I'm on top, in tune, in touch, and going for it!"*

That's how the neural activity feedback loop works, every day, in real life. You decide to think in a more positive, self-directed way. Your brain "gets it" and records your thoughts. When you repeat the same thoughts often enough, your brain wires them into neural pathways, and connects them to other, similar pathways you have already stored. Your brain then sends those same messages back to you as *"thoughts," "beliefs,"* and *"attitudes"* that you act on.

When you repeat those same thoughts, your brain records them—and the positive process continues. When you do that, you begin to create a positive neural network in your brain that will help you change your thoughts, your attitudes, and your actions.

This neural activity feedback loop literally shapes and *re*shapes who you become, and it continues to do so for your entire life. With this discovery, we have the missing link that explains both *neurologically* and *behaviorally* why we do what we do, and how we change—why one life works, and another does not—and what each of us can do about it as we live out our own lives.

The neural activity feedback loop proves that a pattern of success and happiness—the gold-colored brain—is not luck, and it's not limited to something only *some* people get to experience. It's the result of programming and reprogramming positive neural networks into the brain—with *intention*, and with the right messages.

If you think just 35,000 thoughts in a day, and if you live to be 85 years old, that would mean you will think 12,775,000 thoughts a year, or 1,085,875,000 thoughts (that's over a billion individual thoughts) in your lifetime. That's a lot of thoughts. If you start now, think how many opportunities you have to get it right.

Happy brain? Unhappy brain?

Because of neuroplasticity, and what you can do to change your own thoughts and your brain itself, having an unhappy brain, or having a happy brain—will, happily, be up to you.

Chapter 4

The Brain that Changes Every Day

What if you had a brain that was designed to start fresh every morning, could change and grow constantly, would rewire itself with anything you told it, always got rid of the limits other people placed on it, had a potential of reaching a usable IQ level above what you thought you had in the past, was capable of talents and skills you thought only other people had, and would continue to grow and evolve throughout your entire lifetime?

What would you do if you had that brain? *You do have that brain.* That's the brain you were born with.

And yet, some people might ask, "Aren't we born with genes which define us and tell us what our limitations are?" "Isn't our intelligence limited to the scores we got on the IQ tests we took in school?" "Aren't we destined to live out what nature gave us, good or bad?"

It's true that, for centuries, it was believed that the brain was virtually unchangeable after its initial growth period during our youth. (Scientists now know that the brain continues to grow new neurons throughout the lifetime of the individual.)

Though we now know better, until recently most scientists believed that a person's genes controlled the architecture of the brain, and that the brain, in turn, controlled how each individual would think, how intelligent they were going to be, and for the most part, what inborn and lifelong qualities they would or would not possess.

The result of that point of view was that our educators believed we were born with "gifts" or "failings" based on the genes with which we came into the world—with some people seemingly more gifted than others. Our genes, and the role they played in our lives, were thought to be in control of almost everything about us. Even something as important as our usable IQ was believed to be fixed—cast in stone for our entire lives.

It was also believed that talents or abilities we might seem to be born with would usually be the same talents and abilities we would end up with at the end of our lives. And even those talents and abilities would inevitably be diminished by the ravages of time as our brains aged, unable to change or adapt—like the cultural belief that "you can't teach an old dog new tricks"—which we now know is completely untrue.

Many believed our ability to learn *skills* was also clearly limited by the genetic determination each of us was allocated at birth. What we were "cut out for," educators and even parents told us, was the path each of us should follow.

Sharon would be able to play the piano, but Tim wouldn't. Instead of becoming the engineer that he could have been, Johnny's self-image would be that of a poorly-paid mechanic, and his destiny would follow his self-image. Some people would become doctors, while others were told they would *never* be able to do something like that. Some would be entrepreneurs and business leaders, while others would be consigned to the mail room.

Some young people were thought to be better suited to follow a course other than a higher education. The belief was that they would be better off just to develop what few skills they could find on the meager menu life had given them. They would have to learn to be content doing something that was thought of as "less important" than people whose more fortunate choice of genes gave them what they needed to become college graduates. And without the right motivation from their parents and teachers to help them excel, many of them would choose the lesser path.

Whatever skills we would be able to develop, we were told, was regulated by a genetic predetermination that favored some—and limited others. It didn't seem right, of course, but because we were born with a certain set of genes, and were given a certain level of intelligence (which was always less than someone else's), what we were given at birth would dramatically influence or control the outcome of what each of us would make of the life we had in front of us.

It is here we discover the problem that has held back generations of individuals from reaching their greatness:

We have become what we were programmed to believe, instead of what we could have become.

Who Are You Really?

Imagine the choices we've made that have led each of us in one direction instead of another, simply because the teachers, parents, and others who guided us believed the brain we ended up with was the brain we would live with for the rest of our lives—a brain that determined who we were, or who we were destined to become.

Even the simplest off-hand descriptions we hear about any young person are often defined by what we had assumed to be natural traits, personal characteristics that tell us *who* that person is, and *how* that person "will be": *Ricky is stubborn. Carol is shy. Kristen is smart. Jason is going to be an athlete. Laura is a dreamer. Kevin has ADHD and can't concentrate. Josh is a loner. Ellen will never be good at math. Brian is just like his father.*

Each of us was defined by the same kinds of beliefs, and the same kinds of personal and social misconceptions. For most of us, our education was based on preconceived pictures of what our capabilities were, and yet, many of those pictures were *wrong*. The preconceptions about who we were *designed* to be, and who we could become, were based on assumptions about the human brain that were false.

It is true irony that the people who had the most accurate picture of the brain's potential were the visionaries who believed "anything is possible," and that positive thoughts create positive results.

Yet those visionaries—who had a large part of the answer—were often not taken seriously by the educators themselves. (To my knowledge, no school or university at the end of the 20th century had a Dean of Positive Thinking.)

Insight into the lives of successful individuals had convinced those of us in personal growth research that there was a direct relationship between a person's attitudes and beliefs, and his or her probable level of success. People who believed in themselves, for instance, time after time did better than people who continually doubted themselves, or believed they would not succeed.

The educators, meanwhile, followed strict and limiting guidelines, supported by "standardized" tests that failed to recognize the plasticity of each individual brain being tested. Students were classified and categorized, and put into columns of capability, many of which had *nothing* to do with what that student's *true* learning potential or life capability might actually be.

Because of breakthroughs in the field of neuroscience and, in particular, developments in the world of neuroplasticity, the way we test and evaluate children and students is now being turned upside-down. So will be the way we look at every facet of education, from child-rearing to classrooms to textbooks to grade progression, and how we train and educate each individual student.

Your IQ May Be Higher Than You Thought

There is a very good chance you are smarter than you thought. Or, at least, you could be if you chose to be. In a few short years we will not even recognize the standard IQ tests we relied on in the past. (How could a single test, administered perhaps only once during your youth, accurately define the intelligence of a brain that changes constantly and literally rewires itself every day of your life?)

If, as we now know, your brain makes changes based on the input you give it, then it makes sense that if you give it the right, new input, your capable or usable IQ will grow right along with it. At a minimum, the ability to *use* your intelligence more efficiently and effectively, will grow.

Keep in mind that the new understanding that a finite IQ is *not* genetically pre-programmed into you, gives you the amazing opportunity to reset your own usable intelligence. Even now, brain researchers and personal growth trainers are creating brain training exercises that will change the neuronal structure of the brain itself. As this kind of training progresses, it will give everyone who wants to, the chance to become more capably intelligent, and more aware and in touch with everything around them.

An Incredible Opportunity for Parents

If you have children in your life, I encourage you to pay close attention to the work being done in this area. Your children have the potential of becoming as intelligently capable as you help them become.

The positive brain activity of your children is based on the amount of the right kind of stimulation they experience. All children are open minds, waiting to be fulfilled. If you choose to see each of your children as an incredible opportunity to form their minds and their attitudes with the most wonderful, optimistic, creative, searching thoughts and ideas, then you will instill in them the tools they'll need to become the amazing individuals you would like them to be. You will, by your conscious, caring input into their minds, give your children a future of unlimited potential.

It's Where You Want to Go—Not Where You've Been—that Counts the Most

The results of positive programming can never be underestimated. I have seen so many people change their lives for the better, just as a result of getting the right messages often enough and strongly enough that they literally changed their paths in life. And it didn't seem to matter how difficult their circumstances were to start with.

In my own experience, I recognize that few people today would know, when I walk on stage to speak in front of an audience of 10,000 people, that I grew up in what we today call "poverty." They have no idea I might have had no chance at all to achieve anything beyond a lifelong struggle and a future of deprivation and mediocrity.

My early school life was fraught with the intensely-felt embarrassment of wearing clothes that were old and hand-me-down, and shoes that were tattered and worn. I still remember the taunts from my classmates when I had to wear my older sister's worn out tennis shoes to school after she had outgrown them, because I had no shoes of my own. There were eight of us in my family, living in a small house that would have been barely big enough for a family of two.

But we survived. What our life lacked in "physical wealth," my parents and my family made up for in "emotional wealth." Instead of the best clothes, I was given the lifelong apparel of a belief in the powers of creativity, and the possibilities of the future. Instead of being given new shoes to wear, I was given a way to walk forward, and an undying belief in my dreams. In the midst of what others thought was "poverty," my brothers and sisters and I

43

received a wealth of positive mental programs that would stay with us forever. Instead of resignation, we had "will" and self-determination. We were "wired" to go for it and never give up until we reached the goal.

It was because of that early exposure to both the limitations at the time, and the possibilities of the future, that I came to believe *it makes no difference where you came from, if you know where you want to go.*

Why Not Wire Yourself for What You Want?

For you, in your own life now, it's likely you are even *more* than you believed yourself to be.

If you have already mastered self-belief, and are on the path to success and fulfillment in the important areas of your life, with what we now know about wiring your brain to take you there, it's possible there may be no dream that is too big, and no goal you cannot accomplish.

Even if you've dreamed great dreams of your tomorrows, and it's already easy for you to see yourself accomplishing your highest goals, imagine what you could do with those same dreams, if you were to consciously wire them in to the "do it now" action circuits of your own brain?

Most of us received more programs of what we could *not* do, than programs that told us what we *could* do, or what we *could* become. This is true whether you are already a super-achiever, or have yet to live out your full potential.

We *become* most, the way we become *programmed* most. You may have some great programs, or perhaps you have programs that could be working against you, programs you might like to get rid of or change.

Fortunately, because of your neuroplastic brain, if you have something in your programs you'd like to change, beginning now, there is more than hope; there is something you can do.

Chapter 5

Your Neuroplastic Programming

From the moment you were born, every message you received was recorded in your brain. *All* of your perceptions—everything you heard, everything you saw, everything you experienced, every thought you thought, every message you received from any source, was recorded in your brain.

The messages that were repeated, and therefore recorded repeatedly, formed neural pathways and neural networks in your brain. We call these neural pathways and networks *programs.*

The metaphor of the brain being like a computer is accurate, at least enough so that it helps us illustrate how the programming of the brain works, and it makes it easy to understand.

This is especially true of how, like a computer, the brain does not evaluate the accuracy of each message you give it. Can you type something into your computer or portable device that's not true? Of course you can. (Otherwise we couldn't write novels—or political speeches!)

The process in your brain that stores all of those messages you give it every day, accepts anything you tell it. The storage part of your mental computer doesn't know whether what you're telling it is true or false, right or wrong, positive or negative, bad or good. It just stores it, and if the same message is repeated often enough, the brain wires it in and acts on it as though it's *true*.

Neural Pathways are Created by
Repetition . . . Repetition . . . Repetition

In the simplest terms, what's actually happening in the brain is that each repeated message you give to your brain either creates a new neural pathway, or it reinforces a pathway that's already there.

When your brain gets a new message, it will first do a quick search to see how that message fits with other information your brain has previously stored. If it's a new message, your brain will store it, at least temporarily. Then, if that same message is repeated, your brain will begin to form a new neural pathway.

You might compare this process to building roads. In time, in the brain, with enough repetition, pathways become roads, roads become highways, and with a *lot* of repetition, highways become superhighways.

Now imagine that those paths, roads, highways, and superhighways are the actual recorded neural networks that hold your beliefs, your attitudes, and your opinions about everything. Every belief, every attitude, and every opinion you have was created by that same pathway-building process in your brain.

The brain is designed to create those pathways, roads, and highways whether the messages you got that built them in the first place were true or not! They *become* "true," in your mind, because your brain has built a highway, a *program*, layer by layer, that is so strong it now appears to you to be *true*.

It Isn't Your Genes—it's Your Programs

It is not your genes that determine your future. We thought for a long time that our genes ruled our lives. It was generally believed that genetic determination—the genes you were given at conception—played the principal role in who you would be, and for the most part, the kind of life you could expect. That theory held until neuroscientists discovered that your genes are more of a blueprint than a map, and your blueprint is mostly similar to everyone else's.

Research in neuroscience then revealed something else, something startlingly important to all of us. Your genes (your DNA) are like switches that are activated—that is, turned *on* or turned *off*—by your environmental perceptions and, in this case, by your own thoughts. *Your genes are like switches activated by your thoughts.*

That means your genes don't control your life or your makeup or your future. *Thoughts* themselves can flip the chemical switches that turn your DNA *on* or *off*. Moment by moment, day by day. We used to believe we were controlled *by* our genes. We now know we control *them*. And one of the ways we do that is by our perceptions and our thoughts.

48

One person wasn't born with a gene to be unlucky, while someone else was born with a gene to be on top of the world. We don't have a gene that makes us love history or not, dress a certain way, talk too much, like rock music, constantly feel insecure, always be on time, love cars, procrastinate, or have a desire to live an upscale life. Those aren't genes; those are *programs* that get wired into the brain.

In exactly the same way, we have few beliefs, attitudes, or opinions about anything that are truly *ours*. We borrowed most of them. We may *think* we have original thoughts, but only a very few of our thoughts come even close.

What you think about the home you live in, the clothes you wear, the job you have, the people around you, how much you're worth, the colors that attract you, the way you vote, the car you drive, the television shows you watch, the values you hold, the food you like, the books you read, the fears you hold, or the dreams you keep—all are the result of messages that got recorded in your brain, formed pathways, turned into highways, and became your "truths."

You Are the Programs You Have Now

There is no part of your life that escapes these programs. They are a foundational part of every thought you think, and every action you take.

If you were to exist for one day without the programs that make up who you perceive yourself to be, and without everything you believe about your world, for that day you would find yourself in an endless mental and emotional void—with no attitudes of any kind, no mental pictures or ideas to identify who you are, where you've been, why you're doing what you're doing, what's important to you and what isn't, or what you believe about anything.

Without your programs, you would have nothing to ground you. You would have no purpose, no focus, no hopes, no sense of self, and no belief in anything.

Obviously, then, our programs are extremely important. We need them to survive. But what if many of the programs we have are the wrong kind? What if many of them are negative and work against us? The neural pathways in the brain that create our programs were formed by *input*—and not necessarily by *truth*. You and I became the living result of the programs we received, whether those programs were accurate or not.

What we believe right now about anything, and who we are today, is *not* the product of clearly articulated truths that were carefully taught to us, thought by thought and program by program, by all-knowing, perfect guardians.

What we believe about ourselves is the result of messages we have gotten from everywhere around us—parents, family, friends, teachers, television, movies, the Internet, people at work, the music we listen to, the people we live with each day—as our brains work overtime to process and program an endless stream of input from everything we perceive.

That would suggest the questions, *"Are my thoughts really mine? Do I really think anything for myself? Am I really a unique individual, with thoughts of my own? Or am I just a result of the programs I have?"*

The answer is, you have the chance to become *the real you*—the unique, individual you—only when you take charge of your input, and only *when you control your programs*. When you do this, your own free will becomes a reality in your everyday life.

Wiring Your Future Starting Today

When we think of how we're *going to be*, or how we'd *like to be* in the future, every image we see is first filtered through our programs about who we believe we are now, and what our experiences have been—who we believe we were—in the past. Who we "could" *become* is based on who we think we've *been*, and that's based on all of the old programs we have stored up.

So we're seeing old neural circuits of pictures of ourselves that may or may not be true. What if the future "you" is *not* dependent only on the person you've believed yourself to be up to now?

If the outdated paradigm about the brain was true, that the brain itself was unchangeable, then it would make sense that the only accurate way to predict your future qualities and behaviors would be to look at who you've been and what you've done in the past.

But if the neuroplastic brain is continually *changing itself based on the latest information it's receiving,* then the person you thought you were up to now, is not necessarily the most important determinant of the *you* you're about to become *next.*

With what we now know about the brain and its ability to change, it has become clear you can create a future which surpasses the one you might have only dreamed of in the past.

A Visit to the Newborn Nursery

My favorite place in a hospital is the newborn nursery. When I have the opportunity to visit that area, I'm always struck by the miracles to be witnessed there.

Imagine now that you and I are standing in the hallway, or the viewing room, looking through a window into the *future*. There, on the other side of that window, in their little bassinets, wrapped in their swaddling blankets, we see those beautiful miracles of life—new little infants, precious in every way. And if they're awake, and their eyes are open wide, we can actually *see them searching*, looking for that incredible life of unlimited potential that lies in front of them.

It's true, when we see them there, lying securely in their little bassinets, waiting for their worlds to begin, when we look at them, all we see is *promise* and *potential*. Their whole *world*, their entire *life* is in front of them. (No one ever looks at an infant and thinks, *"Loser!"*)

Now let's imagine, as I always do when I see a tiny child, that each precious infant has a little baby keyboard strapped to his or her little infant chest. And like a very special computer keyboard, this keyboard is connected directly to their little infant mind. Above the keyboard is a sign with instructions on it. And it says:

Parents, family, teachers, world . . . I don't know how to do this by myself, so I need your help.

First, I need you to tell me my name, so I know who I am.

I need you to teach me how to walk, so one day I can walk on my own.

I need you to show me which way to go, so I'll always know the right direction.

I need you to show me what I can do, so I'll always be able to do something worthwhile.

But more important than telling me who I am, I need you to tell me who I can become. More important than teaching me how to walk, I need you to show me how far I can go. And more important than telling me what to do, I need you to tell me what wonderful things I can achieve and accomplish with this precious gift of life you have given me.

Above those instructions, there is a yellow and black warning sign that reads:

Warning: Everything you type into this child's keyboard will be stored for life, and acted on as though it is true. Please be careful. *Every message counts.*

That's where it all begins for each of us. We are born with unlimited potential, waiting for our future to happen. If we were able to, at the time, we would hope that everyone around us read those instructions, and heeded the warning. (Unfortunately, children don't come with instructions and a warning sign. It's up to us to get it right.)

Two Different Kinds of Programs

Take a moment and visualize the most *successful person* you can think of. This can be someone you know personally, or someone you know of. The person may be someone you've read about from the past, or someone who is living today. But this should be the person who you believe to be the most successful person you can imagine, not just financially, but successful in *life*.

Get a clear picture of the successful person you're imagining in your mind. Pause for a moment, and clearly visualize that person. Then, once you have the image of that person clearly in your mind, I'd like you to bring that person to "life" in your mind, and have him or her stand just a few feet away from you, off to your right. Whoever that person is, they don't mind being there; that person is confident, self-assured, and happy to help. That person is *successful*.

Now I'd like you to imagine the exact *opposite* kind of person. While the successful person is still standing there, off to your right, I'd like you to visualize someone else, someone who is *failing* at life instead of succeeding at life. This second person could be someone you know, or know of, whose life has failed—and instead of moving ever upward in life into happiness and fulfillment, this person's life spirals downward into deepening despair.

When I ask you to think of a person who is failing, my own mind immediately takes me to the picture of a young person who ran away from home when he was still in his teens. His parents have never seen him again. If he is even still alive, he would be in his early twenties now. If they did find him, I suspect they would find him in an alley somewhere. And if they found him, I doubt he would even

54

recognize them anymore, because of the drugs and chemicals in his system.

That's the picture which immediately comes to my mind when I think of someone who is failing in life. Your picture can be of anyone that comes to your mind, who is failing, spiraling down instead of spiraling up.

Whoever you chose to visualize as someone who is failing, I'd like you to imagine that person standing a few feet off to the left of you. Whoever it is, he or she probably would not want to be there, but for the moment we'll suspend belief and ask that person just to stand there.

You now have two very different people standing near you—one to your right, and one to your left.

Let's focus first on the one on your right, the successful one. Let's listen to that person's *self-talk*—for a few minutes, or a few hours, or a few days. When we listen to that person, we hear words like *"belief,"* and *"achieve,"* and *"imagine,"* and *"goals,"* and *"opportunity,"* and *"potential,"* and *"love,"* and *"hope,"* and *"faith,"* and *"caring,"* and *"Can I help?"* and *"Yes, I can!"*

From this person who is succeeding in life, we wouldn't just hear those kinds of words only now and then; we would hear words like these *often*, again and again, at any time, on any average day.

Now let's listen to the self-talk of the person who is failing. We could listen for a few minutes, or a few hours, or days, and I assure you we would seldom, if ever, hear words like *"belief,"* or *"achieve,"* or *"imagine,"* or *"goals,"* or *"opportunity,"* or *"potential,"* or *"faith,"* or *"love,"* or *"caring,"* or *"Can I help?"* or *"Yes, I can!"*

We would not hear the words of belief and success used again and again from this person. We may never hear them at all. If those words were ever in them, they are gone now, covered over by the negative programs of despair and defeat.

When we look at these two people now, one so successful in life and the other failing, we can't help wondering, "What is the difference between the two of them? *Why is one so successful, and the other one failing so badly?"*

What Makes the Difference?

The difference is apparent in their self-talk! *And their self-talk is a direct reflection of the programs that got wired into their brains.*

It wasn't luck or fate. It wasn't genes or destiny. It was the messages their brains received, from the moment they were born, and throughout their lives, with repetition after repetition after repetition, recorded as though those messages were true.

In time, they, themselves, became their own strongest programmers, with their own self-talk now repeating so well the messages they had received again and again for so long. *Program by program, neural pathway by neural pathway, one of them was wired for success, and the other was wired for failure.*

That is the difference. That's why they live and think and believe so differently today. It was first the programs they received from others, and in time, the messages they repeated again and again to themselves—*their self-talk*—one the good, right, positive kind, one the destructive, doubt-filled, negative kind.

And what is most remarkable, and makes the story of these two individuals so profound, is that the two of them, so different in their lives today, could have been two of the infants we saw in the newborn nursery just a short time ago!

Both of them were miracles of life, lying next to each other in their little infant bassinets, wrapped in their swaddling blankets, their eyes wide open, *searching*, waiting for that incredible life of unlimited potential that was in front of them.

Those two individuals, now so far, far apart in their lives, were born with exactly the same promise and potential. And they could have been born in the same hospital, in the same city, in the same hour of the very same day!

We Can Change the Story

How different the story of the one who failed might have been, had he or she grown up in a different way, fully aware of his or her promise and potential, and always knowing and believing it could never be lost!

Though it is seldom to that extreme, with one person succeeding completely and the other person failing completely, that example shows us how people are born with the exact same promise, then grow up with the contrasting programs they receive, and the vastly different lives they end up living as the result of those programs.

When you were born, *you* were a precious, beautiful infant like they were, an incredible miracle of life, filled with promise and unlimited potential, lying in your little bassinet, your eyes wide open, searching for that amazing future that was in front of you!

Then, life got underway, and life's programs began. Some of those programs may have been wonderful and enriching, while other programs you got may not have been the best. Combined, the programs you received have caused you to become the person you see yourself to be today.

As you grew older, you might have begun to think of the life you have as something that's "just the way it is." But it's *not* just the way it is—or at least, it doesn't *have* to be. Life for you is not dependent on how it's *been*, or the way you thought it *had* to be. Your life *should* be what you want it to be *next*.

The truth is, the promise and potential you were born with, never *leaves you*. It can *seem* like it goes away, but that's just life's problems trying to cover it over, as though daily living could somehow take it away.

You never lose your "promise and potential"—the most important and necessary survival and achievement tools you were given from birth—just because your life has challenges. You were born to achieve and accomplish the highest expression of positive fulfillment, which means living up to your best. The gifts you were born with, *you still have.*

That promise and that potential are a part of who you are, and as long as you're alive, no matter what difficulties or experiences life brings you, nothing can take the gift, the promise, the hope, and the potential away from you. That's your birthright. You had it when you were an infant taking your first breath. As long as you are breathing, your promise and your potential are still yours. You may be surprised to find how much of that gift of you can still bring to life.

You can't change everything about your life, but you can take charge of *you*. You can take charge of your programs, who you are, how you feel, what you think, what your attitude is, what actions you take, and what you choose to do next. *But you have to wire your brain with what you want it to do next.*

Neuroplasticity Means Good News

Fortunately, your fate is not sealed. Your future is not cast in stone by the programs you have now. As we will see, if you have programs that are working against you, you can get rid of them or *change* them.

(The brain gets rid of circuits that are no longer being used. An important tool the brain uses to keep itself running efficiently, with as few unneeded circuits as possible, is called "pruning." The brain will get rid of neural pathways that are no longer being used or are no longer necessary. That's where the term, regarding the brain, *"use or lose it,"* originates. If you have program pathways you want to get rid of, the brain is designed to help you *delete* them.)

If there are better programs you'd like to have, you can have them. If there is a better life you'd like to create, you can create it. That's how neuroplastic programming works. That's what your brain was designed to do.

If you've been working with your own brain and its neuroplastic possibilities for some time, and already have a master plan in place, you'll find the tools we're discussing here will help you climb mountains that are even higher and more exciting, and reach ever-increasing levels of fulfillment and expression in every area of your life. But whether you're

59

just getting started or are well on your way, the power of neuroplasticity will work for you.

Chapter 6

The Programs You Get from the World Around You

When you start to become fully aware of your own programming, one of the first things you notice is the amount of programming you get from the rest of the world.

Your brain's neuroplasticity doesn't automatically discriminate between good, well-chosen programs coming from sources you choose, and the completely random programs coming in to you from everyone and everything else around you. Those programs—including the massive amount of programs you didn't ask for or aren't even aware of—also rewire your brain. The problem is, they wire your brain with a lot of the wrong kinds of programs.

Imagine that every program you got had to be typed into a computer keyboard you carried around with you, and that keyboard was wired directly into your brain. Your keyboard is, in this case, your five senses.

When you're by yourself and in control of the input you get, you can decide what gets typed into your keyboard. But when you step out into the world, the world types whatever *it* wants to type into your computer.

It's as though you held your keyboard *facing out* in front of you, and said, *"Here you go, world. Here's my keyboard. Type anything you want. Program anything you want to program into my brain."* Which is exactly what the world around you does.

Mirror Neurons

The subject of "mirror neurons" and mirror neuron systems may have neuroscientists debating for some time: whether, and where, exactly, these neurons reside in the human brain, how much actual influence they have in our reflexive actions, and what role they might play in other areas of our lives.

In my own observation and study of human behavior over many years, there is clear evidence that we "simulate" the emotions, attitudes, and actions of others. We unconsciously "mirror" the people around us. Many scientists believe this is because of mirror neurons.

Since there is more research that remains to be done, for our purposes here, I'm using the term mirror neurons as simulating neurons—any neuronal activity that simulates or infers the actions, feelings, or intentions of others.

In each of us, our own mirror neurons fire when we're *observing* an action being taken by someone *else—even when we are not the ones taking the action.*

That's so important to understand, I'll say it another way: Mirror neurons in your brain fire—just as though *you* were the person taking the action—even though all you're doing is *observing* the action, as someone *else* takes the action.

When someone smiles at you, your mirror neurons fire in response—duplicating the same emotion in your own brain, without you even being aware of it—and make you want to smile back. (It's also because of mirror neurons that we yawn when someone else yawns.)

The research suggests that mirror neurons also mimic the feelings and attitudes of others, *and imprint those feelings and attitudes into your brain as well.* So it's not just the *actions* of other people you unconsciously respond to; it is also their *feelings* and *attitudes.*

It's our mirror neurons that cause us to cheer when we're watching our team score a touchdown on television, or why we can cry with genuine sadness when we're watching a movie, even though we know it's only a movie. It's because our neurons are also involved in watching the movie—and they cause our brains to react to the movie as though it's real, as though *we're* the one who is living it.

Some scientists contend that because of mirror neurons, the human brain is designed to be a "copycat" brain. That's the brain's way of helping us to rapidly learn what we need to know in order to survive and get through life. But those same copycat brains can also get us into trouble, because they copy and record other people's programs—including their attitudes and feelings—without us being aware of it.

This would explain why, when you're with someone else, your own neurons can mimic the behaviors, moods, and attitudes of the other person, literally putting your own wiring "in sync" with theirs. (Some scientists propose that this is where *empathy* originates: with mirror neurons in your brain mirroring and copying the firing of neurons in the other person's brain.)

What that means is that the programs you receive from the people you spend your time with most, are neither casual nor unimportant. When you're in the company of someone else, your neurons are literally firing and wiring *in concert with* how the other person's neural circuits are firing at the time.

(Interestingly, some neuroscientists refer to the mirror neurons as the "mind-reading" neurons. In some ways, they may be right.)

That's why someone else's mood rubs off on you when you're around them. It also explains that *"feeling"* you sometimes get when you're around someone else. It can be a good feeling, or an uneasy feeling. At times you may not be exactly sure what the feeling is or where it's coming from, but it's there, and you can *feel* it. That's your neurons firing in tune with the other person's thoughts or feelings.

(Most of the "vibes" we get from being around someone else may actually be coming from the sympathetic firing of our own mirror neurons.)

Your brain is, in that sense, *linked to the other person's brain,* with your brain's neurons firing (without you being aware of it) in response to even the subtlest motion, a slight change in a facial muscle, an unnoticed eye movement, and even the smallest gesture or change in the other person's body motion or language.

Your proximity to that person will do that. Your empathy with that person will do that. And over time, the repetition of *their* thoughts and their attitudes will be mirrored by neurons in your own brain and wired in to your brain. That's why we become most like the people we spend our time with most.

Key Point:

Because of the way your brain will unconsciously duplicate neural activity of the person you're with, anyone you spend your time with can imprint your brain with their programs. And, unless you're aware of this, neither of you will know it is happening.

The "Power Programmers" — Who is Typing on Your Keyboard?

Let's consider just a few of the external programmers that have access to your mental keyboard. As we do, keep in mind that the messages you receive, from any source, are *recorded* by your brain—which means that *other people are wiring your brain.*

Here are just a few of your most powerful programmers:

1. Your Friends.

Friends are one of the top sources of programs that get wired into your brain. Friends are the people you *choose* to spend time with, of course. And your brain records their words, their attitudes, and their feelings, just as easily as it records your own. Which should make you question just how qualified a "programmer" each of your friends is.

Ask yourself this question: To which of your friends would you give your mental keyboard for a day, and let them type anything they wanted to type into your brain—knowing that your brain would record it, and could even wire it in if repeated often enough?

Another reason friends are primary programmers in your life is because you listen to them, you pay attention, and greater *focus* creates stronger programs.

The message is immediately obvious: choose your friends with care. Choose who you spend your time with, and be selective about how much time you spend with them. Choose the friends who believe in you and see you at your best, and whose programs you wouldn't mind "mirroring."

Remember, *your friends are wiring your neural networks* (even when neither of you are aware of it).

You may have heard the expression which tells us that "we become most like the five people we hang around with most." The truth is that it isn't just *five* people—it can be many of them, and they are some of your strongest programmers. Now we know why.

2. Your Family.

Your family is similar to the "friends" group, but there are important differences—the first of which is, you get to *choose* your friends. And that means you can *change* your friends. It's much more difficult to get a new family.

Another difference is that while the messages your brain receives from friends may have strong emotional content from time to time, programs from family members are often filled with emotion.

We've learned that *emotion* is one of the mechanisms in the brain by which programs imprint faster and stronger. This means that when a family member says something to you, and it comes with strong emotions attached—*love, joy, anger, sorrow, guilt, hurt, etc.*—your brain is getting a stronger message than just the message of the words themselves. So it wires more circuits, and the program it creates becomes stronger.

Another reason family programs are strong programs is because of the amount of *repetition* of the messages that takes place simply due to proximity and the amount of time you spend together.

In many cases, of course, our families are our positive bedrock, and we are thankful for them every day. If you are blessed with positive-thinking family members, they can be some of the most beneficial, strongly encouraging, and *believing* people in your life.

But if you happen to have any family members who are negative, or who constantly communicate messages you don't want to have programmed into your brain, remember that in the brain, the strongest programs win. So make sure *your* positive programs are your *strongest* programs.

It might be easier if you didn't have to deal with some of the family programs in the first place—that is, if they are negative, or if they are prone to having questionable opinions or attitudes you'd rather not program into your own brain.

But you can counteract some negative input from others by making sure your *own* self-talk and your programs are so healthy, so positive, and so strong that in the war of the neurons, yours will be the strongest programs, and negatives from others won't be strong enough to override them.

When it comes to family members, love each of them, but be aware of who *is* and who *isn't* sharing the best programs.

3. *The People You Work With.*

This is another group of people you may not have much choice in selecting—if they're part of the job you want to keep. The people you work with can also rank high in the amount of programming they create in your brain, simply due to the amount of time you spend with them.

When someone at work has an attitude that rubs off on you, that's mirror programming. The neurons in *your* brain are copying and wiring in *their* mood, whether or not it's the best mood for you to duplicate.

When someone at work lifts your spirits, or brightens your mood, that's mirror programming. And when an associate causes you to become upset or angry, that, too, can be mirror programming—and your brain is busy taking it all in, recording it, and if the situation continues, wiring it in place.

The *opinions, ideas,* and *beliefs* you hear from the people around you, are all *programs.* When you hear those opinions, ideas, and beliefs repeated frequently, you can be sure your brain is busy wiring *their* thoughts into *your* head. If you go through a list of the people you spend most of your time with on the job, this may or may not be good news.

Other People's Opinions

It's clear that we get programmed by what other people say. And there is no greater example of this than the *opinions* that other people so freely give us—that may not be desirable opinions at all for us to have.

With few exceptions, here's a good rule to follow: Unless you ask for them, other's people's opinions don't count. Let me repeat that: *Unless you ask for them, other's people's opinions don't count.*

In fact, when someone gives you their opinion about anything that has to do with *you*, it's actually *their programs about themselves* that are talking to you.

What other people "think" is based on every one of the programs that are wired into *their* brains—and none of those programs is based on you; it's based on *them*. Opinions are *opinions*, and nothing more. Advice from a friend may be well-intentioned, but it is not *your* future, hopes, ideas, and dreams talking to you; it's *theirs*.

How many lives have been hurt or upset just because someone followed the opinion of a well-meaning but unqualified friend? How many goals, great ideas, and possibilities have been dashed on the shores of disbelief, just because someone gave an opinion that had no more value than the mere fact that they thought they had the right to suggest to someone else how that person should live his or her life?

This is about your independence, your personal responsibility, being smart, thinking for yourself, and choosing *your* programs for yourself.

After you become an adult, the only time to listen to *anyone's* opinion other than your own is when you *ask* for the opinion—and then, make sure you consider the quality of the source.

Obviously, you should seek out and find the best counsel and the best ideas from others when you are ready for input. But that is far different from the spurious noise you get when other people, who are often less capable than you, give you their opinions as though what they think is "truth" for you. It often isn't.

No one but you has lived your life. No one but you has had your experiences. No one but you sees your today and your future dreams, aspirations, hopes, and possibilities as you see them. No one can do your thinking for you, nor do they have the right to do so.

The next time someone says, "I think you should do *this*," or "I think you should do *that*," make the conscious choice to think for yourself. Whoever it is, that person is giving you *their* pre-programmed ideas of what they would like you to do. You can listen, but don't automatically accept anyone's picture of what you should do next.

Ask yourself, "*What does my own mind tell me is the best for me, right now, in my own life?*"

Other people's opinions are an expression of their own mental programs. If you like their programs, and ask for their opinion, listen to them, but stay mentally engaged and continue to decide for yourself. Unless otherwise asked for, the most important opinions you will ever listen to will be your own.

4. *Television.*

It's ironic that television programming is actually called *"programming."* When it was first given that name, I doubt anyone knew that one day television would become one of the most powerful programmers of the human brain in the world. When you're watching television, or even when it's

70

just on in the background, your brain is being programmed with every message you get.

With television today, the idea of programming your brain is not accidental; it is by design. Every moment of your television day is created to keep you watching, keep you hypnotized, and keep you buying. (I know—someone is always quick to point out that there are some *great* programs on television. And they always mention the same three or four shows.) But there are endless hours of programming on television that are *not* designed to wire your brain with messages that are healthy and good for you (or your children).

Television programs are designed *intentionally* to wire our brains to respond to their messages in a way that will convince us we need the products their sponsors are selling. And as life-long television viewers, we have been so conditioned to that programming being a "normal" part of our lives that we may never stop, think about what's happening to our brains, and cut the cord.

Other than overcoming the lifelong habit of watching (most people are lost when the power goes out), this one should be easy to fix—but it usually isn't, precisely because television has become a habit that is as wired into our brains as getting up in the morning.

But I encourage you to become actively aware of what's really going on in your brain when the television set is on. The next time you notice the television is on (remember, it's wiring your brain even when you're not paying attention to it), ask yourself:

Why am I watching this?

Is this something I want my brain to record?

If my brain records the thoughts from others, including television, do I want my brain to mirror what I watch on TV?

Is this creating a "positive loop" or a "negative loop" in my brain right now?

Is there something else I could be doing that would be time better spent for me?

If I would like to program my brain in the most positive way, what should I do next?

When it comes to our emotional growth and well-being, television is a pervasive example of programming in its most powerful and potentially destructive form. If you watch too much of the wrong kind of television, your brain has no choice but to record the messages that your television is giving you.

Because of neurons you have which are designed to perceive everything around you, to teach you how to learn and how to live your life, part of who you will become is based on what your television programs fill your brain with most.

5. *The environment of your home.*

Aside from watching television, what are the messages that living in your home gives you? You're not only programmed by the words someone speaks; your brain receives messages from virtually everything it perceives around you. Your home can be a storehouse of memories, emotions, and messages—some good, some not so good.

Most homes have a "feeling" to them, and that, too, is noted and recorded by the brain. You may find that one room is uplifting and makes you feel good, more so than another room. Colors, textures, furnishings, wall hangings, room size and shape, architectural trim and enhancements— everything adds to the ambience of your home that sends messages to your brain.

In my own life, I'm so sensitive to any environment I'm in, that I always make sure any space I'm going to spend a lot of time in *feels* "right." If it doesn't, I change it. Your environmental space can literally change your mood (it does that chemically, in your brain), and it will help you to be aware of how important your space is to your programming.

(Our environment can literally influence our success. We *think* differently in one location or space than we do in another. One can even study courses in how concepts of design, decor, and orientation affect our psyche. The practice of feng shui is an example of this. Many believe that everything in our space and environment affects subtle energies in our central nervous system.)

When it comes to programming and your home environment, keep in mind that your brain is observing everything you do, and a lot more, including all the unconscious messages and signals that come to you from the space you're living in.

Here are some key questions to ask:

How do I "feel" about my home?

Does my home create an attitude that is "up," "neutral," or "down?"

When I am home, how "successful" do I feel?

How does my home make me feel about myself overall?

Is my home a healthy space, both mentally and physically?

Is my space a peaceful space?

Is there anything I could change about my home to make it a more positive place to be?

If you find that a careful examination of your living space shows you it could be wiring you in the wrong way, you may not have to move to a different home to change it. Making even small changes can help. As the most apparent example, put things on your walls that give you uplifting messages. That can be framed pictures that are inspiring, or something as simple as positive quotes that you read online, print out, and post around your home.

The first thing I look for when I'm going to spend any length of time in a living or writing space is what's on the walls. What's on the walls will become what's in your brain.

6. The rest of your mind time.

Your brain is constantly receiving messages from everything in your environment. What you do in your spare time; what you read; if you play video games, the games you choose to play; your hobbies—anything your brain can perceive creates a message of some kind. With each of your activities, ask the question—*is it helping me program my mind in the healthiest and most positive way?*

I'm not suggesting you suddenly change everything you see, think, and do with your "mind time." But if even a few of your chosen pursuits send your thinking and your life in the wrong direction, it's worth the effort it takes to re-evaluate—and then make the necessary changes.

Chapter 7

The Mind that Lives Beyond Your Brain

To help you get a clear picture of how you, the individual you, are a wonderful combination of both your mind and your brain—and how they both cooperate to make you the amazing person you are, we're going to take a look at how your mind and brain work together in your daily life.

To do that, we'll use the metaphor of the brain as a personal computer. But to understand the power of neuroplasticity, this time we're going to look at your computer brain in an important new way. This view of your computer brain has four parts: the basic computer, the software, the computer operator, and the silent controller.

Picture #1. **The Basic Computer**. This represents your **physical brain**.

The mental computer itself, and its internal memory storage, is where the permanent programs that manage the computer's operating system are stored. The computer, with its programs, *does not actually think for itself.* It just records and stores the programs it has been given, and its operating system acts on them. Your basic computer is your physical brain.

Picture #2. **The Software**. This represents your neural pathways and circuits we call "**programs**."

These are the programs of information (experiences and perceptions) that are added to the software library your computer has been storing since before you were born. They interact with the hardwired programs in the computer's memory storage. Software programs can be temporary or permanent.

In the brain, our software is made up of the neural pathways and circuits in which, among other things, all of our beliefs are recorded. These beliefs can change as our experiences change. Through repetition, these belief pathways become stronger, and more "permanent." In time, they can become so strong, they appear to be hardwired into the brain.

Picture #3. **The Computer Operator**. This is *you*—the "you" that you're aware of. This is your **conscious, thinking mind**.

This is your "thinking" mind, the part of you that's consciously reading this book right now. This is the self-aware part of yourself that you live with each day, that you see as the "real" you. This is the sense of self you wake up with in the morning and go through the day with, and it's the you that you're conscious of before you fall asleep each night. Some people, especially those who are not aware of brain processes, believe that the conscious, aware "you" is the *only* you.

The reason many people perceive this to be the only "you" is because this is the part of you that's able to consciously enter new messages into your brain's software. Put another way, this is the you that "thinks."

Each of us has a miraculous quality of the conscious mind that's able to *override* previously stored programs in our mental software, and create new decisions which are made seemingly independent of, or *in spite* of, our old programs.

Because of this ability of your conscious mind—through your *thoughts* and your brain's neuroplasticity—you are able to reprogram your brain and create new neural pathways. This is accomplished by the conscious selection and direction of your thoughts, repeated often enough for your old patterns to change.

Picture #4. **The Silent Controller**. This is your brain on **autopilot**.

Your computer has *two* operators: Your conscious mind, and your silent controller. One is the mind, your conscious, active, thinking mind. The other is an invisible *synaptic neurological process* that goes on behind the scenes, within your brain—choosing, selecting, and making thousands of your choices for you, day in and day out, and as a result, literally voting on, determining, and creating the life you live each day.

This silent, invisible operator is your brain on autopilot, the part of your brain that actually makes most of your decisions for you. It sets up your feelings, and predetermines your actions and unconscious responses.

Your "Silent Controller" Makes Decisions for You—Without Asking You First

This invisible, unthinking, silent controller that sits with you at the keyboard of your own mental computer is made up of all of the thousands of neural pathways and networks your brain has previously recorded and stored.

These decisions are made by an unconscious process that is controlled by the number and strength of the programs you have on any given subject or attitude, and whether your programs are positive or negative—which simply means whether they work *for* you or *against* you.

As an example, what do your programs tell you about how comfortable you are speaking in front of a group? The more prerecorded programs you have that tell you you're *not* good, or *not* confident, or *not* charismatic when you're speaking in public, the more those programs will vote *against* you the next time you even *think* about standing up to speak.

But on the positive side, the greater the number of previously recorded strong programs you have that show you a picture of yourself that is confident, articulate, well-liked, and persuasive, the more those programs will vote *for* you the next time the opportunity comes up to speak publicly.

Your "Subconscious Mind" is Your

Brain's Neurons Silently Firing

While there is a faculty of the brain is referred to as the "subconscious mind," it's not actually a part of the *"mind"* at all.

Our more recent understanding of the brain suggests that what is called the "subconscious mind" is actually a result of the neural activity of the *brain itself*—your brain's neurons silently firing, without your control or awareness—rather than being a part of the activity of the *"mind."* In fact, the process can take place without the *brain* discussing it with the *mind* at all.

This silent controller is a purely physical, chemical, electrical response activity that takes place in the brain as a result of stimuli that the brain is constantly receiving, sorting, and acting on, without the conscious mind being aware of it. Look at the silent controller like your brain taking an invisible vote on most of what's going on in your life—and acting on the results—without you even being aware of it.

A Bird's-Eye View of Your Autopilot in Action

To get an idea of what your brain's processing center does and how your silent controller operates, let's pay it a visit. During our visit, you'll only be witnessing the surface activity that's obvious, but take note of everything you see.

This is the place where your millions of neuronal circuits, pathways and networks are wired. Pathway by pathway, neuron by neuron, connection by connection, program by program, this is where all your *beliefs, opinions, attitudes* and *thoughts* about yourself and everything else in your life are stored.

This is where your important memories live, but this is also where every random program and unimportant memory you have ever wired in is stored. (Not every memory gets wired in; many unimportant memories just go by the wayside. The difference is in the number of times those random programs or unimportant memories are repeated.)

To visit this amazing processing center, let's imagine you're standing on an observation platform above this vast network of neural circuits. From our vantage point, we're going to observe three different examples of your brain in action.

To start with, you'll notice that here and there, like fireflies of electricity, different neural networks are firing and sending their messages to other neural networks. They're communicating with each other. They're monitoring your physical body and every perception that comes in from your environment. They're working at their primary goal: they're keeping you alive.

This is where 90% or more of your choices are made. It's where your beliefs, opinions, and attitudes are stored— everything you think about you, and everything you believe to be "true." *It is here that your programs live. It is here that your programs vote on every unconscious decision you make.*

It's your autopilot, and it's not only able to keep your body functioning automatically, but by constantly sorting through the thousands of programs it has stored, it's also able to keep most of your *thinking* on autopilot as well.

Now, as you're standing on the platform above this vast landscape of neural circuitry that makes up your brain—

81

watching some circuits fire while others remain dark—you want to see an example of your brain in action. To do this, you shout the words, *"Help! I'm in trouble!"* as loud as you can.

Suddenly, the instant you shout the words *"Help! I'm in trouble!"* the sea of neural circuits lights up brilliantly, with clusters of networks flashing and connecting with other networks in the vast array of neural circuits below you.

What's happening is that your brain is *talking to itself* at high speed, searching for any information it can find that will tell it what's wrong, and what it needs to do to make sure you're safe. It's also sorting every file available from your past experience, so thousands of neural networks are talking to each other at lightning speed, while your brain is alerting your "fight or flight" control center that there could be trouble.

In all of this, as soon as you shouted *"Help,"* your brain, entirely on its own, went immediately into action, scanned files, checked programs, virtually *re-read your past* and started sending messages to your conscious mind. And it did all this in a few heartbeats.

Giving Your Brain a Single Word

That was just one picture of your brain at work. Now, let's look at a second picture.

Sometime later, after things calm down and your brain is quiet again, and not too much is happening, we're going to have you do something different. You're still standing on the observation platform watching your brain's neural networks quietly glowing with activity here and there.

But now, for your second test, instead of shouting an alarm of any kind, you simply say one random word. You say the name *"Jane."* You don't shout it; you just say it quietly, once: *"Jane."*

In seconds, as soon as you say that one word, you notice that the neural networks below you suddenly light up! Some of them even connect with other networks in a completely different part of the brain map beneath you. It looks like lightning is running throughout all of your brain's neural networks, making sure that every reference of any importance you've ever placed on the name "Jane" is being consulted and evaluated. If that value is great enough, it's being sent upstairs to your conscious mind, to make sure you're aware of the connection.

You may have read some Dick and Jane books in early childhood; you also knew a girl named Jane in third grade and another in Middle School who you thought was a really fun person, and you liked her.; you remember a reference to the term "plain Jane" in a book you read a while ago; and you recently watched an anchorwoman named Jane on a television newscast.

As you stand on your platform now, the mass of neural networks below you are deciphering, comparing, and analyzing every reference you've previously stored on the single word "Jane." You can see your brain light up, brightly in some areas, more dimly in others, into the infinite horizon of the brain landscape you see beneath you.

Your subconscious brain has just analyzed every word, every name, every thought, every picture, every feeling, every nudge, every uncertainty, every memory of every stored experience you had that was connected to the word "Jane," and played it out on the brain map we just saw.

What this tells us is that *a single word or thought will light up the connections in your brain*, without you even knowing that the connections are being made.

With that in mind, let's look at a *third* moment of connections in your brain.

Sending Your Brain a Message of "Self"

In this example, let's say your brain has quieted again, and let's watch what happens when we do something else. This time, you're not going to shout an alarm or quietly say the name Jane. This time, as you're standing on the platform, watching how your brain will light up next, you say the words, *"I believe in myself, and I know I can win!"*

Now your brain's neuroprocessing center lights up in dozens of areas, searching, looking for context, finding every single message you have about the words *"I believe in myself, and I know I can win!"* along with every *similar* program you have that is connected to them. Your brain lights up!

What your brain's neural network search is looking for is everything you have previously stored about you, your belief in yourself, every triumph you experienced in the past, how confident you are in the outcome now, and your belief that you can accomplish the goal.

Every significant program your brain finds in that search will be delivered to your conscious mind. It will, in *seconds*, begin to present you with messages from every cluster of neuron circuits you have ever stored which agree with your statement, messages that tell you that you can *win*.

In each of the three examples of looking in on the brain (*"Help! I'm in trouble!" "Jane,"* and *"I believe in myself, and I know I can win!"*), what's important for you is that each time, the stimulation your brain received ignited your usually unseen subconscious brain with neural activity, some of which came to the surface as messages to you. You then act on the strongest messages you get—without ever really having to "think" about it.

In your everyday life, this is what your brain is busy doing all the time; you're just usually not standing on a viewing platform watching it work.

Your Autopilot is Making Decisions for You

To show you how this works in your everyday life, let's say you're at lunch and you're trying to decide whether you should break your diet and have the Death by Chocolate for dessert. You may think a brief thought or two about it, such as *"Hmmm, let's see, should I order the chocolate cake or not?"* But before the decision comes to you consciously, it's actually being made *for* you, *unconsciously*, without you even knowing your silent controller is making the choice.

Here's what's instantly happening in your brain: Hundreds of prerecorded neural programs made up of your beliefs about your diet, your weight, needing comfort, deserving dessert, what your mother might have told you as a child, how well the day has gone for you so far, and countless other pre-programmed messages that are all connected to the choice you're about to make about whether or not to order the dessert—all those programs *vote*, silently and instantly. The vote is counted, and the results are collected by your brain, which delivers the verdict to your conscious mind.

Autopilot: *The dessert wins.*

That same process goes on, dozens, hundreds of times in a day—so invisibly, so *unconsciously* that you're not even aware the voting is taking place. Unless, of course, you stop, really think about it, *consciously* intervene, override your past programs, and choose the outcome of the vote for yourself.

Key Point:

Most of your brain's programming and most of your decision-making—90% of it or more—is handled on autopilot by your silent controller—without you being aware of it!

Overriding the Autopilot

We live in a world filled with the non-stop rush of work, 24-hour television news, and more day-to-day demands and responsibilities than we were designed to handle. Our minds are bombarded with the chatter of turmoil and chaos—the unfiltered input of everyday life.

We're so busy, we're on autopilot most of the time. We multi-task so much of the time that we feel guilty if we're focusing on only one thing, or getting only one thing done. We are harried, harassed, and hassled. We pray for a quiet day, and then we put it off for some other time.

We often give no more thought to who we're really meant to be, and what we could truly accomplish with our lives, than we give to what we will wear to work in the morning. And we're somehow able to do all that without stopping to think about it, or wonder what we're doing it all for.

That would be a pretty depressing situation, if not for what we've learned about the plasticity of the brain. We now know that from the moment you decide to take control, your *mind* has the power to change neural networks that control your attitudes, actions, and feelings, and even the neural networks that control your "personality" itself—something we used to think was lifelong and unchangeable. You can override the unconscious autopilot mechanism—by *choice*—and create new neural networks of your own choosing.

Your "Mind" and Your "Brain" are Not the Same Thing

As you can see, when it comes to living your life, making countless choices, and getting them right, your *mind* and your *brain* are two very different things.

Because the goal is for you to take as much control over your own neuroplasticity and programming (and thereby your life) as possible, it helps to see the brain and the mind as separate entities. They work together, but they have very different responsibilities.

Scientists disagree on where the "mind" is, exactly. The reductionist view sees the mind as being nothing more than the end result of brain chemistry—a view that is being challenged by quantum physics, and perhaps, neuroscience itself. The more we learn, the more it appears that the mind manages the brain, and not the other way around.

For our purposes here, we're going to view the mind as being something outside of, or apart from the physical brain, but working synergistically *with* the brain.

The reason we look at it this way is that the *mind* can do things that cannot easily be attributed to the physical brain itself:

It is your mind that is aware and self-aware.

It is your mind that is creative, gives you inspiration, and is the inspired and inspiring you.

It is your mind that sees beauty in symmetry and sunsets, and is moved to write sonnets.

It is your mind that consciously chooses to love.

It is your mind that sees beyond the everyday electrochemical computer chatter of your physical brain, and shows you your true potential and purpose.

It is your mind that reminds you of your greatness, and reminds you that you were born with unlimited promise.

It is your mind, not your brain, that is the visionary you.

It is your mind that is the you that hopes and dreams.

It is your mind that is the you that chooses to have "faith."

It is your mind that sees far beyond the three pounds of "gray matter" that your brain is composed of, and it is your mind that shows you a greater purpose, far beyond procreation and survival, in the meaning of life itself.

Your brain doesn't do all that. Your *mind* does.

With this understanding, we change from the powerless and pointless attitude that tells us *"Life is life, and you have little or no control over it,"* to the far more practical attitude of *"Life is what you choose to make of it. How would you like it to be?"*

This is where "free will" comes into the picture. It is when you use your conscious mind to exercise conscious control over the autopilot and exercise your *free will* to do so, that you actually put your true "self" in control.

From the neuroplastic point of view, the mind controls the brain—or at least, it *can*, and it *should*. Does that mean you can create your own future? Yes, it does, and yes, you can.

There is a very specific process to use when you want to override your autopilot and create more of the results you want in your life. Next, we will learn exactly how to do that.

Chapter 8

The Seven Rules of Neuroplasticity
The Rules for Wiring Positive Programs

In the previous chapters, we've discussed how neuroplasticity works, some of the influences you face every day, the importance of mental programming in your personal growth, and the powerful role your autopilot plays in creating your day-to-day life. Knowing that, what can you do about it?

One of the most helpful things we've learned about neuroplasticity is that there are specific rules to follow, if you want to deliberately wire your brain with the right programs. Practicing these rules helps those programs to be imprinted more rapidly and lastingly.

These seven "rules of neuroplasticity" will help you deliberately take control of your thoughts, your programs, and their outcome in your everyday life. They come to us from studies in neuroscience in which researchers have identified the basic requirements for improving neuronal growth.

All of these rules *work together* and complement each other, so you get the best results when you pay attention to all of them. If you follow these rules, set goals, and program yourself for positive results, you will begin to get more out of your life and your dreams than you may have ever thought possible.

The seven vital elements for wiring positive programs are the following:

1. *Mindfulness*
2. *Choices*
3. *Intention*
4. *Focus*
5. *Repetition*
6. *Emotion*
7. *Belief*

All these elements have to do with how the mind and the brain interact to create new programs. *All of them begin with what takes place in your mind*—so to apply them, you *think* about them. The result is that you consciously help your brain create and store more of the programs you want.

Another reason to actively practice these seven rules is that when you do, you're no longer leaving the programming of your neural pathways up to randomness, or up to your brain's old programs. Applying these rules puts you in control. When you're in control, you're able to create programs that are healthy, strong, and positive, and they'll be the programs that *you* choose. With the right programs, the right *actions* will naturally follow suit.

91

To acquaint yourself with the seven rules, answer the questions in this short questionnaire:

1. *Am I being consciously* **mindful**? *Am I always aware that my thoughts are programming my brain?*

2. *Am I making my* **choices** *consciously, or are my old unconscious programs making them for me?*

3. *Do I know exactly what my* **intention** *is? Do I know exactly what I want? Do I know the goal?*

4. *Do I* **focus** *on my goals, and on the programs I want to create?*

5. *Am I using* **repetition** *to create the programs I want to create?*

6. *Am I adding positive feelings and* **emotion** *to the programs I'm creating?*

7. *Do I have strong, positive* **belief** *in the outcome?*

Asking yourself those questions frequently will help you recognize and practice the most important rules of neuroplastic programming. The more you're aware of these seven elements, the more you think about them and practice them, the more quickly you'll take personal control of your programs and begin to change them, along with changing the actions you take.

This is an enlightening introduction to the process of rewiring your brain. When you practice the seven rules of neuroplastic programming, you'll begin to discover what you and your brain are actually able to accomplish *when you work together.* You'll be able to notice a difference in who is really in control of your brain almost immediately.

You'll also find that none of the seven rules is difficult to practice. Mastering all of them is worth it, and all of them count. Remember, repetition creates habit—and the whole point is to get your autopilot, which controls your unconscious choices and actions, working *for* you instead of against you.

The description of each of the rules and how to best apply them, as I've outlined them for you in the following chapters, will help you master each of them.

Chapter 9

Rule #1 — Mindfulness
The Vital Role of *Awareness*

This rule is *very* important. Being "mindful" will have an immediate and positive effect on how well you do at wiring your brain in the right way.

As we're using it here, mindfulness is the process of being consciously aware of your own mental environment and activity in a purposeful way, at all times. It is your self-directed awareness of your own mind and what you're doing with it.

Mindfulness, in these pages, is "paying attention to paying attention." It follows a form of active thinking called "metacognition"—which, in the brain, is a function of the prefrontal cortex—and helps you regulate and manage your own thoughts. It has to do with thinking about, consciously, what you're thinking about.

It is mindfulness that first tunes us in to taking charge of the programming of the brain. When you'd like your brain to do something special for you, the more attention you give to what your mind is doing, the better you'll be able to direct your brain to help you accomplish it.

Perhaps the far opposite of mindfulness is being "absent minded"—as though your mind is absent—such as when you walk into a room, and then can't remember why. Or you find yourself standing in front of the open refrigerator, and have no idea what you were going to get from it. We often say in situations like these that "our mind was elsewhere," and that would be true.

With mindfulness, your mind is right *here*, and on high awareness. Being highly aware creates an electrochemical state in the brain that alerts it to—and keeps it mindful of—your objective.

This self-aware mindfulness sets up the working environment your brain needs for it to follow your directions without the usual background noise and static that occurs in your brain when it is receiving no specific directions from your conscious mind. A randomly rambling mind is not a self-directed mind.

As we'll see later, while it may be the *choices* you make each day that determine the road you wish to follow, it is first your mindfulness that heightens your brain's sensitivity to seeking that path. When you're practicing mindfulness, you're saying to your brain, *"This is important to me. This is something I want you to be aware of and work on with me."* Or, *"I'm about to set a goal, and I want you to help me reach it."*

In the broader sense of being mindful, you're increasing your general awareness of the natural programming process of your brain. You become more aware, minute by minute, throughout each day, that you and your brain have a partnership. You tell it what to do, and with repeated direction, your brain begins to wire it in.

When you regularly practice becoming consciously aware, several things happen:

1. When you're mindful: *You are aware that every message you give your brain is being recorded.*

This one step of mindfulness alone can change how you think, and what you say when you talk to yourself. By focusing on your own awareness, you begin to change the underlying programs that direct your thoughts and words, because you're aware of them at all times.

When you think a thought, its direction will be either negative, neutral, or positive. As we discovered when we were "coloring" the brain, the thought could be described as *a)* a thought that works *against* you or your well-being in some way, *b)* a neutral thought that has no positive or negative value ascribed to it, or *c)* a thought that works *for* you in a healthy, productive way.

If you really should be exercising, as an example, the simple thought, *"I should exercise today, but I'll put it off until tomorrow,"* would be identified as a "negative" thought because it works against your well-being by stopping you from following the healthy exercise schedule you set for yourself. The thought, *"I choose to exercise today,"* would be a "positive" thought because it helps you stay with your exercise plan and take the action that is healthiest for you.

In the past, unless you've already been practicing mindfulness, this process has, for the most part, been unconscious. That means your thoughts and your self-talk have been being created by old programs, good or bad, that were already in place.

When you practice mindfulness, you begin to create new thought-directing programs which override previous programs that may have allowed you unconsciously to move toward the negative instead of the positive. And with mindfulness, your brain will actually begin to prune out the old negative neural circuits that are no longer being used, and get rid of them—just like a gardener would prune out the old branches on a rose bush, so the new roses will have more room to grow.

When this happens, as you're continuing to practice your new awareness and are more conscious of your thoughts more of the time, even your *unconscious* thoughts will automatically begin to move toward the *positive.*

2. When you're mindful: *You are aware that your choices change your programs.*

The more you're aware that your choices themselves play a role in wiring your brain and creating your programs, the more important each of your choices becomes. Mindfulness helps you keep your choices in front of you. It gets you to ask the question, *"Is this a good choice, a neutral choice, or a bad choice?"*

What you do next, as a result of that choice, will be recorded by your brain, and when that same choice is repeated, your brain will start to wire it in—the beginning of a new program, and a new habit.

3. When you're mindful: *By being more aware of your programming, you create stronger programs.*

Being mindful of your programming not only allows you to control the input; the mere addition of your *awareness itself* adds chemical strength to the neural pathways your brain is forming. Being aware of your programs makes them stronger. And because you're aware of the programs that are being formed, you're able to direct the process, making sure that you're sending the most positive, most healthy, most productive messages to your brain—instead of something less.

4. When you're mindful: *You're aware that the objective you're working on at this moment is something that is important to you, and you want your brain to pay close attention.*

It is mindfulness that sounds the wake-up call to your brain. When you practice mindfulness long enough for it to become a habit, you'll find that even when you're in situations when you're relaxed or not trying to focus intently on the moment, you'll suddenly hear yourself tell your brain, *"This is important,"* or *"Here's how I choose to think about this."* That will happen when something comes up that really matters to you. And it will happen because you have created mindfulness programs that keep your awareness closer to the surface.

5. When you're mindful: *You improve your memory.*

When you hold your attention on one thought for even 10 or 15 seconds or more, in a state of focused mindfulness, you upgrade that thought from short-term memory storage to longer-term memory storage. When you're playing catch with a baseball, it isn't enough to let the ball hit the glove; you have to catch it and hold it. Putting a thought into long-term memory is like that; you have to catch the thought and hold on to it long enough for your brain to keep it.

What Happens When You're Not Being Mindful?

When you're *not* practicing being mindful, you're saying to your brain:

1. *I really don't care what program pathways you set up for me today. I'm too busy to notice, and I'm too busy to be mindful.*

2. *I hope you lead me in the right direction, but I'm going to leave it up to you.*

3. *I'm going to leave my unconscious choices for today up to the old programs you have recorded—even the negative ones.*

4. *I have decided to rely on luck to get me through.*

None of that sounds either intelligent or safe. Remember, *you're* in charge; your brain isn't. It's your job to be mindful, make the choices, set the course you want your brain to follow, and stay mindful throughout the day, every day.

That can sound like a tall task, and one that's never-ending. But keep in mind that mindfulness itself is also a habit that becomes programmed. The more you practice doing it, the more natural and automatic it will become. In a short time, being mindful can become as natural as listening

99

to someone when they're talking to you. It becomes a natural part of your life, every day. And it creates an awareness and a sense of being in control that almost nothing else can match.

"Habits of Distraction" Are the Opposite of Mindfulness

Look out for things that seem to be harmless, everyday distractions or habits that can go unnoticed. They're a part of our lives, and seem normal, but are the *opposite* of mindfulness.

In most homes, the number one habit of distraction is television. As I've said, watching television is designed by its producers to be a habit, and most television viewing, as far as your brain is concerned, is mind*less*, not mind*ful*.

In some homes, the television is the first thing awake in the morning and the last thing to shut down at night. Many people don't pay attention to it or watch it, but it's still on in the background, and in your mind it's drowning out any chance of mindfulness or any kind of awareness at all.

Another habit of distraction that hinders mindfulness is idle conversation filled with gossip. I know, we're all social creatures, and we need social interaction. But if you analyzed the last 10 phone calls that included gossip, would they be *mindful*, positive experiences?

The problem with idle conversation (as opposed to uplifting, productive discussion) is that it is so much a habit, practiced over years, that it pretends to be an essential part of life. Thoughtless conversation isn't really essential at all. In fact, it can be a negative habit, instead of a positive one.

What can a habit like that do to your brain? The programming you can get from the one habit of idle conversation mixed with spurious gossip is frightening. Fortunately, it's a habit, and you can *choose* to eliminate it from your life.

A third habit I'll mention, that can take the place of mindfulness, is the Internet.

The number of hours a week people spend on social networks alone is astonishing. I would only recommend that if you want to be mindful, you will have to be aware of what you're doing with your mind *now*, and then decide if that's what you really want to be doing.

There is no "positive programing angel" hovering over us to keep us from filling our brains with all the wrong stuff, and spending our time, instead, being mindful and aware. You'll have to do this one for yourself. But you *can* do it. Being mindful is fun. And making it a positive habit is an important part of taking control of your life.

When you pay attention to your mind, you might really like the person you're getting to know.

Chapter 10

Rule #2 – Choices
Taking Control of Your Programs

When you're changing your brain, choose thoughtfully what you want your brain to record.

The subject of choices and how we make them is so important that I wrote an entire book, entitled *"Choices,"* on the subject.

The reason choices are so important is that without making clear choices, you leave your brain to its own meanderings—and those are determined by your old programs or by the random influences of whatever happens to be taking place in your life at the moment. In either case, that's not always the best course to follow.

It makes sense that if you want to set up healthy neural pathways for your brain to follow, since your thoughts and your actions play a major role in the programs your brain is creating, you should make choices that create the right programs. That includes both the choices you *think* about, and the choices you *don't.*

102

Your choices affect your programs, and your programs affect your choices. Each choice you make gets recorded in your brain, and if you repeat that same choice often enough, it will actually form its own set of neural pathways and connections in your brain. That's how habits are formed. But every choice you make is first influenced by the programs you already have. Here's how it works:

Two Kinds of Choices

We make choices every day. All of them fit into one of two categories: *conscious* choices or *unconscious* choices.

1. *Conscious choices.*

Conscious choices are the ones you think about while you're making them. Your major life choices, you think about a *lot*—choices like where to go to school, what career path to follow, who to marry, where to live, whether to buy a home, or what kind of car to buy.

Those kinds of choices get a lot of your attention because they require a commitment, so you think about them, you study them, and you seldom make them quickly. Those are *conscious choices*, and you're aware of every one of them you make.

A step down from the major life choices, but still conscious choices, are the kinds of choices that deal with what you do during the normal course of a day. You consciously think about everything from what you're going to do Saturday night to when to wash the car or what to have for dinner. None of these are life-changing events, but you consciously think about them enough to make an aware decision about them.

What those—and hundreds of other greater or lesser choices you make in a day—have in common, is that in each case, if even for a moment, you consciously *think* about the choice you're making, and you're aware that you thought about it.

2. *Unconscious choices.*

Just as important, or often, *more* important, than our conscious choices are the *unconscious* choices we make—and we make hundreds of them in a day. These smaller choices are vitally important, because they make up the countless small steps we take that lead us either *toward* the objective, or *away* from it.

This is where the "silent controller," which we talked about earlier, plays an important role. Research has shown that when we're making each minor choice, our brain activity indicates which choice we're going to make *as much as several seconds before* we come to the conscious conclusion ourselves!

That means that the neural pathways in your brain—your *programs*—know the results of your choice *before you do.*

Any decision you make that you don't *think* about making, is being made *for* you by your brain—which silently consults with the thousands of pre-programmed neural networks you have stored there. Unless you consciously override it, whatever those neural networks tell your brain to do, it will follow. Before you're even aware of it, your neural networks have voted, your brain has made the choice, and you act on it.

What's troubling about this is that it means your choices are being made by program pathways that could be the *wrong* programs—and often are. I've written previously that as much as 77% of all our programs are false, counter-productive, harmful, or work against us.

This means that for the average individual, three-fourths of the programs doing the voting on the unconscious choices the person's brain is making each day, are negative programs that vote for the wrong choices!

Who's Doing Your Choosing for You?

Every day, in every choice you make, conscious or unconscious, your programs are voting on what to do next. The important point is, *if you allow the wrong programs to do your choosing for you, you can't get the right results.*

The value of being mindful of your smallest choices is that by doing so, you take the control over each of them away from the unthinking, silent controller that could otherwise sabotage you. *Something* makes the choice for you in everything you do—from how often you smile in a day, to whether you arrive at an appointment on time, or whether you'll get needlessly upset over a phone call that didn't make any difference anyway.

One of the goals of this book is to help you take back the control of *all* of your choices from any misdirecting programs that should never have been there in the first place—the programs that all too often make your choices for you without stopping to ask you what you think. And what *you* think—*really* think—is what counts most.

Chapter 11

Rule #3 — Intention
Setting the Goal

Intention is a powerful and essential rewiring tool. Intention is the creation of direction, with purpose: it is identifying the goal. In general use, the word intention refers to the act of planning to do something. But here we have an even more important way of looking at it.

Before scientists were figuring out neuroplasticity, we learned from authors writing in the field of physics, the idea that the outcome of certain quantum experiments were proving to be influenced by the *intention* of the person conducting the experiment. Somehow, *thoughts* were affecting the outcome.

Today, experts in many disciplines, such as the field of positive psychology, recognize the importance of intention. When intention is made a part of therapy, it proves to be an important force in directing people's lives as they move forward.

When I train life coaches as part of my work with the Life Coach Institute, the coaches are trained to help their clients take life-changing steps forward by using *intention* and goal-setting as their focus. Whereas, previously, people who were dealing with obstacles in their path, might have consulted a therapist who spent time revisiting, frequently, the problems of the past, they now go to a life coach who helps them look *forward* (intention), instead of dwelling on the past.

When you're rewiring your brain, your success will depend on your mental direction and on the amount of intention you create in your own mind. That force *will* affect the outcome. From a strictly neuroplastic point of view, when you repeat the same intention frequently, you are literally wiring your brain with a new direction, and telling it what you want it to do.

Speaking to the Wheat

We've all seen intention work its power in people's lives. It played an important role in my own life, even before I understood how powerful a force intention could be, and how it could literally create the future.

When I was a young boy, I worked in the farm fields of the Midwest. From the time I was 5 or 6 years old until I was 18, I virtually lived in the fields. Every day throughout the summer, I spent all my time by myself, working in fields of wheat, oats, flax and corn.

When I was 9, I had a dream to one day become a speaker. So to occupy my mind while I spent endless hours in the fields, with the vision of my dream strong in my imagination, I practiced *speaking*. Day after day, entirely alone, with the wheat fields as my only audience, I practiced.

I practiced every gesture, every motion, as I spoke to the wheat. To this day, I have no idea what I said, but I know I learned how to speak, how to gesture, how to pause, how to stand, how to move, how to listen, and how to respond. I learned all that from countless hours of practice, talking to no one but endless fields of golden wheat. If anyone had seen me gesturing and pacing, speaking to the fields, I'm sure they would have thought, "There's that poor crazy kid again, talking to the wheat." But, fortunately, there was no one else as far as the eye could see. It was just me and the wheat.

From time to time, a breeze would come over the wheat field while I was speaking, and when it did, the wheat tassels would rub together, bristling softly in the breeze. It sounded just like applause. It was like the wheat was listening, and applauding in approval.

A few years ago, long after I had left the wheat fields and had forgotten about them, I was speaking to an audience of several thousand people in a huge arena in Poland. While I was speaking, I would pause after every two or three sentences to allow the interpreter time to translate what I was saying. This gave me the opportunity to listen to the audience and its responses.

It was during one of those pauses, while I was standing on the stage, that I heard it. The audience had begun to clap, and the applause slowly built until it filled the huge hall. But what I heard, as if from the distant past, was the sound of a breeze moving slowly through a field of wheat. All of the tassels were moving together, and they were nodding in the breeze and applauding their approval. I was back in the wheat field in my mind.

109

I had gone from the boy to the man, and the boyhood dream had come true. My practicing in the wheat fields was the result of a picture I had put in my mind of one day speaking to multitudes of people. I had no idea at the time how that would come about; all I knew was that I had a tremendous desire to speak in a positive way.

I did not know when I was 9 years old that *I was setting the goal.* My *intention,* reinforced by my constant practice in the fields, was so strong that it literally created my path without my even being aware that the journey had begun. Looking back at the road I followed, it's very clear. But at the time, my brain was faithfully working on the task and attaining the goal, without my conscious mind even having to know the goal was being reached.

Intention and Creation

Let's say there's something you would like to do or achieve. It could be anything—traveling abroad, mastering a star-tracking telescope, starting a new business, going back to school, reaching a goal at the gym—anything you'd like to accomplish. So you focus on that idea, and you give it a lot of energy. You don't do this just once; you think about your goal again and again, day after day.

Over and over, you picture the goal in your mind. After a short time, you begin to see yourself actually reaching your goal, and each day, the picture of the realization of your goal becomes clearer. You find yourself each day making choices, including the little choices that help you define and take steps that will bring you closer to making your once-imagined goal a physical reality.

And then one day, right on schedule, your ship comes in. Your goal becomes reality. You did it! You created it. *You imagined it, you dreamed about it, you formed it in your mind, you focused on it, you took the necessary steps, and you reached the goal.*

Meanwhile, while all this was going on, what was actually happening in the programming center of your brain? Let's take a look:

First step: You created the idea in your mind. The moment you did so, your brain recorded it. It didn't act on the idea yet, but your brain got its first alert about the idea. If the goal was to travel abroad, this is when you put the first travel posters in your mind.

Second step: You thought about your goal often. Now, each time you thought the thought, your brain recorded it again. But by now, your brain had decided to give this idea a special pathway all its own. It became easier to think and *act on* your repeated thought.

(Stated more technically, this is true because your repeated thoughts myelinated and connected existing neurons in your brain. The myelin sheath on those neurons helped speed up the conduction of the message—like installing a thicker, faster cable for the signal to move through. The myelin helped the neurons in that pathway use less energy than unmyelinated fibers, so the message acquired more speed and signal strength.)

By your level of interest and energy, you had signaled your brain with one of the most important messages it ever receives: *Intention! Intention! Intention! I intend to do this. I want to do this. Help me accomplish this.* If your goal was to own and master a star-tracking telescope, this is when you selected the telescope you intended to buy, and started to imagine yourself focusing on the Andromeda galaxy or one of the Magellanic Clouds with your new telescope on a starlit night.

Third step: You didn't stop. You continued to think about the idea and imagine the results. By now your brain not only created a potential superhighway for this new idea, it also began to introduce you to *other* nearby highways in your brain that were going in the same direction—that reinforced your thinking and helped you get there. If your goal was to start a new business, this step is when your brain begins to pull together and reorganize the entrepreneurial and creative skills you already have wired in, in line with your new goal.

Fourth step: The problems and the obstacles that tried to get in the way began to crumble. Your intention, by now, was getting stronger. At this point your "new idea" neural pathways were growing daily and, soon, because of their strength, they became the strongest programs you had on the subject. If your goal was to go back to school, you're setting your schedule to begin.

Fifth step: The new highways your brain was imprinting and recording for you had now, through repetition, grown to be strong new highways of interconnected neuron pathways in your brain. The more you thought it, the more you believed it. And the more you believed it, the more you thought it. If your goal was to bench press 50 more pounds at the gym, your reps are now creating more strength, both physically and mentally, and it's working.

And so, in each case, your brain created a positive cycle of repeated, self-directed programs which recreated the goal so vividly in your mind that your brain got the picture, has actually wired that picture in, and continues to work on it.

Without you noticing, your brain formed and reinforced the intricate stream of endless connections, neuron by neuron, axon by axon, dendrite by dendrite. This process creates pathways so powerful that one day you wake up ... and out of nowhere, you have reached your goal.

That's what *intention* will do for you. *Intention is the driving force of creation.*

Chapter 12

Rule #4—Focus
The Power of Detail

If you want to get your wiring *right*, you have to focus. In neuroplasticity, when the brain is rewiring itself, it responds best to clear, specific directions, not to messages that are vague and unfocused.

This is why you get better results when you know what you want, than when you're uncertain about the desired outcome. Saying, "We're going to Disney World on July 4th" does a lot better job of getting you there than saying, "We ought to take a trip this summer." But real focus is even more detailed than that.

You help your neuroplasticity work best when you're absolutely certain of what you want to achieve, down to the smallest detail. This is why specificity and focus are so important to any goal you want to reach.

People who want to make changes that are "general" may do okay; they may achieve something better than they would have achieved had they not set the goal in the first place. But they'll never reach the successes they could have reached if they had spent more time focusing on the specific *details* of the goal they wanted to achieve.

With most of the goals you set, the ones you're most likely to reach are the goals that have the most detail assigned to them. This is true because the clearer the picture you're able to give your brain, the more detailed the neural imprint of that goal will be recorded in your brain.

Make Sure Your Picture is in Focus

Focusing a camera on a distant object describes this exactly.

Let's say you want to buy a house. So you decide to take a picture of the house you want to buy. The first picture you take is taken from a distance—say, five or six blocks away. It's close enough that you can see it's a house, but not close enough to make out the details. The picture of your goal that you give to your brain is a distant, out-of-focus picture of the home you want to own. Your brain records this picture, but almost immediately, you can tell your brain isn't giving you much help in finding ways to get it. In fact, your brain *can't* act on it—it doesn't really know what it is!

So you reset the goal to get the home. But this time you decide to give your brain a clear, sharp picture of your goal. To do this, you take another picture.

This second picture you take of the house is different. Here, you take a close-up of the house, filling the camera frame, and it has all the details: the roofline, the pillars on the portico at the front door, the number of panes of glass in each of the windows, the color of the shutters, the height of the chimney, the pattern of the brick facing, and so on. You've adjusted the focus so that all of the details are crisp and sharp. You follow that picture with dozens of shots of the interior, every detail of every room from every angle. It's a perfect set of pictures; you can see everything. And you can literally see yourself living there.

Since you have a goal to one day purchase this home, you want to give explicit directions to your brain to begin helping you reach that goal.

By studying the pictures you've taken, focusing clearly on the goal, the details of what you want is being downloaded into your brain! *Now your brain knows exactly what you want.* This time, your brain imprints the clear, sharp pictures, and immediately goes to work helping you come up with ways to reach your goal and get the home.

That example is more fact than illustration. Your brain, when seeking a goal, will record only what you tell it, and exactly what you tell it, and only as completely as the picture you present to it. Anything you leave unclear induces the brain to come up with its *own* version of what it thinks you want. That means your unconscious programs could be directing the brain with any *wrong* pictures you might have stored there. You definitely don't want that to happen.

Many people fail to give their brain a clear picture of their goals, either because *a)* they don't *have* a detailed picture themselves of what they want, or *b)* they don't know how to go about detailing the picture they want to give to their brain.

Here are my recommendations on how to create a detailed picture of your goal, and give it to your brain:

Step 1. Research your goal.

Arm your brain with all the facts. Learn everything you can about it. Look it up on the Internet. Is your goal to choose a vacation location? Is your goal to lose weight? Do you want to make stained glass windows for your den? Do you have a goal to fly an ultralight aircraft?

There is virtually no subject you can't find information about, in exhaustive detail. The objective is to know everything there is to know about your goal as you take the next steps.

Step 2. Write down your goal.

Write it down on paper, by hand. The reason I recommend you write your goal by hand is that when you put pen to paper and write the words in longhand, you are engaging more of your senses and creating more neuronal activity in your brain. You're also putting more focus, concentration, and intention into the goal itself. It makes your goal more personal and important.

(If you'd rather write your goals using a keyboard to type them into a computer document or a goal-setting program, that's o.k. The most important thing is that you commit your goals to paper.)

When you write it, describe your goal in detail. If there are details you're unsure of, go back to Step 1 for more research. You can never have too much knowledge about a goal. Write it down. Your brain is reading everything you write.

NOTE: There is a one-sheet format for writing out goals that I've used for years. It's very simple and very effective. You can download and print copies of the goal-setting form at: www.shadhelmstetter.com/goals.

Step 3. Talk about your goal.

The reason it helps to talk about your goal is that every time you discuss it in the right way, you're seeing again the mental pictures you're giving to your mind, you're filling in more detail, and you're combining detail (*focus*) with *repetition*, with *emotion*, and with *intention*.

Never discuss your goal with a critic who can do nothing more than find fault with your goal and try to convince you it won't work. (Sound familiar?) It can be good to ask for outside input, but never from a negative "disbeliever," and only *after* you have your desired idea pictured clearly in your own mind.

I cannot stress this enough. Too often, the excitement of a new goal causes people to talk about it too soon, and to the wrong people. Then the dream dies, poisoned by ignorant and uncaring *words*, when if the fragile new goal had been treated more carefully, it could easily have grown and blossomed into a beautiful reality.

Discuss your goal only with other people you trust, and who will *not* criticize or find fault with the idea itself. Then add the positive words of encouragement and support from those who believe in you, and you're on your way.

Step 4. Visualize your goal.

Your brain sees what you clearly *imagine—as though it is the real thing.*

The practice of visualizing goals was one of the first success techniques popularized by personal growth advocates more than 50 years ago. But the concept is brought completely up to date with our newer understanding that your brain actually wires in neural pathways, based on what you visualize.

Key Point:
What you visualize clearly, your brain sees as real.

If your goal isn't an object or something material, visualize pictures of you in the situation of living out your goal—having lunch at a sidewalk cafe during your vacation in Paris, running in the marathon, getting the phone call from your agent telling you that you just got a publishing deal, sitting in the auditorium as your son or daughter crosses the stage at the graduation ceremony—imagine being there, and fill in the details. Your brain is watching everything you're clearly picturing in your mind, and wiring it in as though it's real.

The more you visualize what you want your brain to help you achieve, the more it sees it as already happening. You are practicing that reality in advance in your mind. Each time you do, your brain is recording it as an actual experience, and making the neural pathway stronger and stronger, even before you actually realize the goal itself.

In the Pascual-Leone Harvard study of two groups of volunteers practicing a five-finger piano exercise, at the end of a week of piano practice sessions, both groups of

119

volunteers showed an increase in neuronal growth in a specific region in their brain's motor cortex. This neuronal growth was the direct result of practicing the piano exercise for a period of time each day.

Here's the exciting part: one of the groups of volunteers had practiced playing the piano *only in their imagination,* without touching a piano! And they achieved results that were similar to those who had physically practiced on real pianos. Their practiced *visualization,* by *itself,* caused the new neurons to grow!

The results of Pascual-Leone's study prove, once again, that the brain wires in *imagined* activity in the same way it wires in actual *physical* activity.

Focusing the *Energies* of Your Thoughts

Something else happens when you decide to focus on what you want. You take "this" much energy (spread your arms out as wide as you can), and put it "here" (bring your hands together and touch one point on the desk or something in front of you). Focusing is about taking a lot of energy, and focusing all of it on one finite point.

A clear example of the power of focused energy is that of sunlight through a magnifying glass. You go outside on a sunny day and sit on the grass. You touch the grass in the beautiful sunlight, and the grass feels soft and cool. In fact, it's a cool day. You have a magnifying glass with you. As an experiment, you hold the glass, which is only two or three inches in diameter, a few inches above a section of grass.

120

Within moments, because it's collecting the sun's rays, the magnifying glass focuses those light rays on a small point in the grass, and it takes only seconds for the focused rays of the sun to turn the point of grass from smoke to flame.

A collection of just a few inches of sunlight, focused by a piece of glass, turns the cool green leaves of grass into a fire of intense heat, in seconds. That is accomplished by energy being focused.

Thoughts are Energy

When you want to imprint clear, strong messages, programs, or *goals* in your brain, it requires the intense focus of your thoughts. Your thoughts are like the sunlight, being focused by your goals. The more of your personal energy you bring into intense focus, the stronger the imprint will be. Your success depends on the *strength* of the neuroplastic programs you imprint in your brain, and you create that strength by the intensity of your focus.

This is why the greatest achievers we have known have said they were completely dedicated to their goal and focused on reaching it. No matter what their goal, it got down to their mental focus—the focused energy each of those achievers added to their intent, created pathways in their brain that were so strong they could overcome any obstacle they encountered.

Your achievement will be determined by the amount of focus you apply to the goal. Reaching goals is based on *neurons*. Success is *neurological*.

121

Chapter 13

Rule #5 – Repetition
How Pathways are Formed

We've seen in the rules of programming we've covered so far—*mindfulness, choices, intention,* and *focus*—that each of those rules is vital to your success in rewiring your brain. But the next rule, *repetition,* stands above all others when it comes to success in almost anything you do.

Your brain forms almost *all* of its new neural pathways through repetition. It also strengthens older pathways with the same process. When I'm asked to give my opinion of what really forms the foundation of success of any kind, my answer is, *"Repetition, repetition, repetition."* That's how the brain works. That's how success works.

Even as you're reading this book, I've used selective repetition to help you wire in and retain the information you're reading more easily. As an example, something that is especially important will be focused on several times throughout the book, often viewed from more than one perspective. This makes key points more understandable and memorable. It takes advantage of the way the brain reinforces *retention* by creating stronger neural pathways as a result of the repetition. The more familiar something begins to feel, the more "permanent" the thought has become.

It is through repetition that you learn, and through repetition that you make the unfamiliar, familiar. And it is through repetition that you create most of the neural pathways that you have stored in your brain.

That's true of everything from muscle memory for athletes, to learning multiplication tables in math, to how to drive a car without having to think about it. "Second nature" is created entirely though repetition.

It's also why practice makes perfect—because it is by wiring the *right* neural pathways in the brain over and over again, that what we're practicing becomes a "permanent" new part of the brain's circuitry.

It was through repetition that we got most of our mental programs and all of our attitudes in the first place. That's why we believe what we believe, and that's how we got the pictures of ourselves that tell us who we are today. The primary tool of neuroplasticity, that forms all of our programs, is repetition.

How did we learn the words to songs we heard when we were young, and learn them so permanently we still know them word for word today? We learned them by hearing them day after day; we learned them through repetition.

What about our eating habits—what we like to eat, and how much we eat? Our eating habits were created by our choices of what we eat, and how much, being wired and rewired into our brain over and over again. We eat the way we eat because of repetition.

It was through repetition that we wired in *all* of our habits: what time we get up; what we talk about most; whether or not we procrastinate; what makes us happy; how fast we drive; how we dress; how we comb our hair; how quickly we answer the phone and how we answer it; how organized we are; what we do in our spare time; how well we take care of our health; our manners and how polite we are; what upsets us and what makes us happy, and every one of the hundreds of other habits each of us has.

Key Point:

It is through repetition (the brain's principal tool of programming) that you will make any future improvements in yourself, or change your habits in any lasting way.

Each time you send a repeated message to your brain, you're applying another, reinforcing layer of pavement to that specific neural roadway. You're sending nutrition and energy to that pathway, stimulating it, and making it stronger.

The use of repetition is a powerful tool your brain requires to move a thought or experience from *"momentary,"* to *"long term,"* to *"permanent"* memory storage.

For now, let me repeat: the underlying secret to creating almost all neuroplastic changes in your brain, is repetition.

Chapter 14

Rule #6—Emotion
The Secret Ingredient

This is another rule of programming that will begin to help you as soon as you begin practicing it. When you're wiring your brain, strong *emotions* create strong *programs*.

Your neuroplastic activity is strongest when your emotions are the most intense. Your emotions create a chemical fuel that ignites programming activity in your brain.

If you want to wire your brain with a new program, add your *feelings* to your goal. Emotions are powerful chemical messengers in the brain, and one of the strongest imprinters you have on your side. Because of this, when you're actively and consciously rewiring your brain, *you will wire in most what you care about most.*

To prove the point of how strongly your emotions imprint the brain, take a moment and think about something that happened to you when you were young, something that still stands out vividly and indelibly in your mind today. As you bring that memory to mind, it's easy to see that it's all still

125

there. It only takes moments to come up with the kind of image that all you have to do is think of it briefly, and the entire memory, complete with the emotions that imprinted it, comes flooding back to you in all its detail.

One of my own unforgettable memories is of something that happened to me when I was 6 years old. Because of the emotions it created in the moment, it stayed with me forever.

I was attending a family reunion, and I was sitting on a dock that reached far out over the water on a wind-chopped lake. It was a dock that stood high above the waves, and the water beneath the dock was deep.

I was sitting on the dock next to my father, who was talking to five or six other men, uncles of mine, who were all sitting on the dock, enjoying the day, and just talking. I was wearing my best Sunday pants and sweater, sitting on the edge of the dock with my back to the water. While I was listening to the older men talking, I accidentally leaned too far back, and I fell backwards, into the deep water. This was especially bad. I didn't know how to swim! The water was deep, and I was wearing heavy clothing that weighed me down.

At this moment today, the scene is so vivid in my mind that the old emotions come rushing back, as they say, as though it were yesterday.

My eyes were open as I saw the water rush over me, and as I sank deeper and deeper I saw the streams of sunlight, darkened by the cloudy green color of the water. The huge posts that held the dock were thick with algae, and while I was trying not to breathe or gulp in water, trying desperately not to panic, I tried to use one of the posts that held up the dock to pull myself up toward the sunlight through the water above me. But my hands kept slipping on the green slime on the post, and instead of pulling myself higher, I continued to slip down, deeper into the dark water beneath me, and I began to realize I was drowning.

I remember calling for help, in my mind. More than anything in the world, I did not want to drown.

Why are those desperate moments stamped so clearly into my brain today, more than 50 years later? Because the experience was charged with such high chemical emotions—in this case, *surprise, panic,* and *fear*—that the event was immediately and *permanently*, chemically, imprinted in my brain.

The brain does that to protect us. One of its jobs is to keep us mindful of things that could harm us, so when one of those dangers comes along, the brain goes on high alert, and puts all of its resources into doing two things: *a)* keeping us alive, and *b)* recording the event permanently so we'll never forget it, in case it, or something similar, happens again.

I should add the other bookend to my story. I'm not sure how I got out of the water—and to this day, I have no idea how I got back up onto the dock. The dock was too high for me to reach, and the slippery post was too slick with algae to pull myself up to get out of the water. But somehow I got out. I always thought an angel must have helped me.

I found myself once again sitting in the same place on the dock that I had fallen from, next to my father, who was still talking to the other men sitting there. He didn't even know I had been gone. I sat next to him, too frightened to speak, soaked, shivering and shaking, water running from the drenched Sunday clothes I was wearing.

My father, who had not noticed my absence, or that I had just almost drowned (and would have been gone forever if an angel hadn't saved me), turned, and finally noticed me, looked down at me and said, "I thought your mother told you not to get wet!"

Emotions are Powerful Programmers

This instant super-recording process in your brain works the same way for you when anything extremely wonderful or good, or something new or different, or otherwise important happens to you—like getting your first bicycle, or your first day at school, your first driving lesson, or a time when you were very embarrassed; when you got hired, when someone proposed to you, or when you did just about anything that was emotionally charged—and therefore, unforgettable.

Those things stayed with you, not necessarily because they were actually important in your life—some of your unforgettable experiences were important, and some weren't—but because the highly emotional content created chemically-charged messages in your brain. Knowing that, it makes sense that if you want a *new* program of your own choosing to also be strongly imprinted and recorded, you can help the process by adding emotion to the messages you give to your brain. When you add strong positive feelings, your brain goes into higher gear and thinks, *"Got it! This is something I'm supposed to remember for a long time. It must be important. So I'll wire it in as 'unforgettable.'"*

Mastering this important tool of the brain will help you wire in stronger programs. But it also explains why your personal attitude—your *excitement* and *enthusiasm*—are so important to wiring your brain in the right way.

Positive Emotions Create Positive Wiring

Adding strong emotions to your intentions can seem difficult at first. That's because we're not used to creating positive emotions by design. We're used to experiencing these emotions as a *result* of something that's happening *to* us, or something we're experiencing in our lives. (It's easier to create the feeling of *anger* than it is to create the feeling of *joy*—and actually *feel* it.)

The problem is that unless we're experienced in meditation, or are trained to be equally successful in *creating* emotions, such as in method acting, almost none of us have very many neural pathways already in place in our brains, to create positive emotions for us.

If I were to suggest that you "feel joy," you can think of things that brought you joy in the past, but your brain doesn't automatically recreate the depth of that feeling for you just because you want it to. If I suggest, "Now, feel enthusiasm," you can understand the *idea* of being enthusiastic, but your brain doesn't automatically deliver the *chemical emotion* of enthusiasm to you. There's a reason for this.

There is a part of the brain called the amygdala, which is designed to alert us to danger. From that part of the brain, we get many more "danger" signals than we get "safety" or "happiness" signals. The brain is designed that way, to keep us alive and safe. (In earlier times, it was more important for

129

us to be fearful of predators in the wild, than it was for us to feel safe and secure.)

Although that same part of the brain also registers positive feelings, it's more important, from the brain's point of view, to always keep us alert to problems or danger, and less alert to the safe, comfortable feelings we're looking for. (That's why we have more negative programs than positive programs. Our brain puts us on alert to notice problems and things that could go wrong, far more often than it alerts us to things like contentment, happiness, and joy.)

This means that, while you probably already have plenty of fear, anger, and angst circuits, unless you've learned how to wire your brain for more positive emotions, you may not have a lot of extra "happiness," "enthusiasm," or "joy" circuits already wired into your brain.

I should also add that when we're angry, our effective IQ goes *down*—which is why we make so many bad decisions and stupid mistakes when we're angry.)

If you don't already have as many positive circuits as you'd like to have, you can wire them in. But instead of focusing only on today's problems, you'll have to aim your thoughts in a new direction.

When you're rewiring your brain, and you want to have the power of positive emotions helping you wire, use your best memories and your most positive dream pictures to create the emotions that will give extra strength to your goal.

Try this Simple Exercise

Think of something you'd like to change or something you'd like to accomplish. It can be anything you'd really like to have happen.

First, get a clear picture of that goal in your mind. Then, while you're thinking about the goal, say the words,

"I love this goal! I can do this! I'm going for it, and I can reach it!"

Now, say the words again. And this time, if you can, say them out loud, and with lots of energy and enthusiasm! While you're thinking about the goal, say the words,

"I love this goal! I can do this! I'm going for it, and I can reach it!"

Think about how great you feel about your goal, and how important it is to you. Raise your shoulders up, lift your chin up in determination, take a strong, deep breath, see yourself being successful and reaching the goal.

Then, while you're still thinking about the goal, and you have it clearly pictured in your mind, repeat the words one more time *with as much feeling as you can*:

"I love this goal! I can do this! I'm going for it, and I can reach it!"

This time, see yourself getting an award for your accomplishment, and imagine hearing a huge crescendo of applause you're receiving for reaching the goal!

If you were to do the simple exercise of focusing on that one goal and repeating those words several times each day for several days, you would start to notice that by doing nothing more than repeating words—*with strong emotions attached to them*—the goal would become stronger. The brain is a chemical organ, and emotions in the brain are chemical stimulators that both affect your feelings, and tell your brain how to react.

The power of self-directed neuroplasticity grows even stronger when you add emotions to the process. And because positive emotions lift you up, while negative emotions pull you down, it makes sense to add the intensity of positive feelings to every good idea you have, and every important thing you'd like to accomplish.

Positive emotions such as *joy, love, peace, harmony, positive expectation,* and *enthusiasm* cause neural pathways to form faster, and also to connect with other neural networks that were formed using similar kinds of positive emotions. (In your brain, like attracts like.)

Creating Positive Emotions

How do you add positive emotion to your brain's programming process when you want to create programs which are especially strong and especially positive? Here are some steps to help generate the right emotion:

1. *When you're reading your goal, or even thinking about it, always think the most positive, uplifting thoughts along with your goal.*

Check your state of mind. If it's not in the most positive place, immediately use self-talk that directs your attitude to find the good and fill you with a feeling of strong positive possibilities.

Pay special attention to your feelings. The more passionate you are about your message or your goal, the more you will wire that passion to the program you're creating.

2. Visualize. Picture yourself not only reaching the goal, but actively imagine yourself celebrating, or sharing your joy with others.

When you *feel* your success, your brain will feel it along with you. Imagine hearing the cheers of applause, getting the warm hugs, or the smiles and handshakes. Do whatever it takes for you. Literally see and feel your triumph.

As I've said, the brain doesn't emotionally identify the difference between clearly imagining something and actually doing it. When you mentally see yourself achieving your goal, you're sending chemical messages to your brain that record those images as being real—complete with positive emotions attached.

3. Describe your goal or idea in detail to people who believe in you.

The purpose of this step is to attach strong feelings—*yours*—to the images you're creating in your mind. Do this with the express intent of getting fired up about what you want to achieve. Instead of describing your vision timidly, or hesitantly, fill your description and the story of your future achievement with passion and enthusiasm! The more *emotion* you *give*, the more *wiring* you'll *get*. And the positive words you'll hear from your "believers" will only add fuel to the fire.

4. Sell yourself on your goal! If you aren't personally sold on the goal, you probably won't achieve it.

133

Selling yourself, with strong emotion, increases the strength of your programs. Go over, again and again in your mind, the benefits you'll create by reaching your goal. Put your strongest feeling into it. List all those benefits so clearly that you literally convince yourself how important it is to reach this goal, and how you'll benefit immensely from its achievement. Go someplace by yourself, describe your goal and its benefits out loud if you can, and literally sell and resell yourself on whatever it is you want to change or achieve.

5. Use music to create emotion. When you're imagining, planning, or taking action, play music that is rich with positive emotion, and is inspiring and uplifting.

I've used music for years to create the precise emotional setting to help my mind work in complete harmony with whatever it is I'm working on at the moment. For most of us (unless we are accomplished musicians), music bypasses the analytical mind and connects us directly with our emotions.

Music can form a strong foundation for attitude. As a result, when the right music is used as the background to your ideas, your thoughts, or your vision, it literally wires those thoughts, ideas, and visions together with the emotions the music is bringing to life. (That's why, in movies, the musical score can be as important as the scene itself. The music uses your emotions to imprint the dialogue and visual images more strongly into your brain.)

It's well worth the time it takes to seek out and find the right music to use as the soundtrack to set up your attitude, and to use for the wiring in of your programs. Find completely new selections of music if you need to. The stronger the emotions you create, the stronger and more indelible the programs you will wire into place.

6. Get up and move.

Use *physical motion* to improve your mental state and create more positive emotions. Do several push-ups, walk around the block, run for a distance, do an aerobic workout, or dance! When you want to add more strong, healthy emotion, get more physical. Sitting in place or doing nothing almost never creates enthusiasm. Strong, positive, physical motion instantly adds an emotional lift.

Positive Emotions Will Help You Win

When you practice applying strong feelings to what you want to change or accomplish, always keep in mind that when the brain is rewiring itself, it *loves* emotion.

Whether you're thinking super-positive thoughts, actively visualizing yourself winning, describing your goal to your believers, selling yourself on your goal, getting your adrenaline pumping by physically working out, listening to inspiring and uplifting music, or all of the above, remember that the emotions you're building will supercharge your brain.

Because of the mental chemistry of your own emotions, the programs you're wiring in will be stronger, last longer, and keep you moving in the direction of achieving your goal.

Chapter 15

Rule #7—Belief
The Quantum / Spiritual Element of Success

*I*f *you want to achieve, make sure you believe.* This is one of neuroplasticity's most important rules. When it comes to wiring your brain, *belief* makes a profound difference in the strength of the neural programs you create.

Key Point:
People who believe in the positive outcome of their goals do better than people who don't. They create stronger neural circuits than people who don't believe in the outcome.

The effects of "belief" on the outcome of goals could be the result of a mechanism of quantum physics, or it could be the result of spiritual energy on the part of the individual setting the goal, or both.

The evidence suggests that when we strongly believe in the outcome of the goal we're setting, we tap into a higher level of awareness, and it is our connection to that super-consciousness that creates a more harmonic continuity

136

between us and our goal. In so doing, we align our physical energies with a higher level of energy.

Materialistic science, which doesn't accept the idea of spiritual or non-material intervention in our daily affairs, isn't sure what to do with the evidence that *belief* changes the *outcome*. And yet, experiments in quantum physics show that the human mind *can* influence the result of the experiment.

Buddhist monks, now famously studied by neuroscientists, have been shown to literally change their body chemistry in carefully controlled tests, while the subjects practiced dedicated forms of meditation. Even more important, they have shown that their meditation specifically causes an increase in the growth of new neurons and neural connections in their brains!

Whatever its source, belief creates an energy that we cannot ignore. And it's a fact that when it comes to wiring the brain, belief counts. When you add *belief* to any goal you set, *something physical happens in the neural structure of your brain. And something measurable changes in the outcome.* Belief *works*, no matter what you believe the source of its power to be.

For those of us who study success, the results of positive belief are too obvious to ignore. (If you had two equally qualified teams, for instance, and one team believed it would win and the other team believed it would lose, which team would you vote for? If you had two equally qualified individuals in *any* endeavor, and one of them believed in a positive outcome and the other did not, which one would you vote for?)

The more that researchers study the emerging world of brain training and neuroplasticity, the more it becomes apparent that belief itself is an *essential* ingredient in successful, self-directed neuroplastic programming. If you want to succeed, time after time, you should consistently add your personal *belief* to the formula.

Belief is a Choice

When you want to reach a realistic goal, you don't have to automatically have faith that you're going to reach it; you can *choose* to believe. At any moment, you can decide, *"I choose to believe."* Sometimes, that's all it takes to get started. (It's also very good self-talk.)

Or you may apply three of the rules of neuroplasticity programming together: *choice, belief* and *repetition*—by using the kind of self-talk that says: *"I choose to believe. I choose to believe. I choose to believe."*

The more you believe in the outcome, the more that outcome tends to happen. When all the other factors are in place, your own choice to *believe* can cast the deciding vote.

Chapter 16

The Noise

There is an underlying layer of brain activity we all experience that is called "mental noise." It is made up of random thoughts and feelings that are just at, or under, the surface of our consciousness. The problem is that much of this "noise" tells us what we "cannot" do in our lives, instead of telling us what we "can do."

What is this noise, and where does it come from? It is the processing part of the brain, endlessly monitoring and communicating our thoughts and programmed beliefs back to us. Sometimes we're aware of the mental noise. Most of the time, however, we sense it, but don't quite hear it or listen to it clearly enough to identify what it is.

When those random, often disconnected thoughts keep cropping up, stop for a moment and listen to them. They're not your higher self, but they are a high level of neural programs that are strong enough to make their way to your conscious mind. When you listen to them, you can decide which of them you want to keep, and which of them you want to change.

139

Listening to "The Noise"

Because of the louder noise of everyday life—not only your own conscious thoughts, but everything that's going on around you—you will often be unaware of the mental noise that's going on below the noise level of life. The time you will probably notice the mental noise most is when you're trying to go to sleep at night. You lie there, eyes closed, waiting for sleep to come . . . and then you hear the noise.

Your mental noise comes in as though someone has just turned up the volume on the most random thoughts that could possibly go through your mind. They're often odd and disconnected—fragments of thoughts and ideas that seem to come from a Pandora's Box of pictures, memories, questions, worries, hopes, and meaningless impressions of vague, unknown images. In what is known as the "hypnagogic state," the time between awareness and sleep, you can experience a parade of unconnected thoughts and images that eventually lead you into sleep.

Another time you notice the noise is when you want to quiet your mind completely, as you do in meditation, or when you want to get in touch with that quieter, more peaceful part of yourself. Sit silently for a short while, relax, and tell your mind to seek *quietness*. Unless you're a practiced meditator, it can feel like someone left the front door of your mental house open, and every uninvited thought you can imagine has come rushing in. (In meditation this is called the "monkey mind" because of its similarity to mindless chatter.)

The source of the "noise" is your physical brain running on autopilot, working without your focused attention. The noise is normal; everyone experiences it and, except for now and then, you may not even pay attention to it. The problem is, much of that noise tends to be *negative*, and it can create a whole host of fears, self-doubts and problems.

When you listen, feel, and experience the mental noise, you're actually looking into the storage and processing center that is home to all the programs your brain has stored, the same processing center we visited earlier.

The only time this "brain on autopilot" pauses and lets you think for yourself is when you become consciously aware and *mindful*—when you pay conscious attention to each of your thoughts, and make conscious decisions for yourself. For the rest of the time, the pre-recorded neural programs that are stored in your brain do your thinking *for* you.

The background noise of your daily life is the part of the neural activity that makes it to the surface of your consciousness. And there's a lot more like it going on below.

What Does the Noise Tell You?

The most important questions here are, "What do your unconscious programs say?" "What makes up the unconscious noise level of your life that is created by the neural recordings you have stored?" And more important to you now, "What do you want your brain to program into those endless neural pathways that end up as the "background" programs to your life in the future?"

Do the background messages of your life that you hear in your mind tell you that you are strong, confident, and capable? Or do those constant flits of noise and half-thoughts tell you that you are something less than that?

141

The noise you're hearing is the result of the programs you have stored—usually for years—in your brain. And as we've seen, this is important because it is those hidden, subconscious programs that are silently doing the voting—and actually making 90% or more of your choices for you.

Changing the Noise

If you think about the picture we saw previously, when we were standing on the platform looking over the complex neural networking process of your brain, it's not hard to understand how many of those past programs become reactivated by any experience or thought we have now that strikes a similar chord.

Because of that neurological process in the brain, the problem we *had* is, in our minds, the problem we *have*. It stays with us as stored programs in the brain. Because the brain, with its stored programs, "remembers" it as being real, our mind once again "sees" it as being real, right now.

Now, by understanding the brain's neuroplastic ability to change, we have both hope and promise that old programs do not have to live with us forever. It is possible and natural, neurologically, to wire your brain with what you *can* do, instead of what you *can't*.

Chapter 17

The Neuroscience of Self-Talk
The Scientific Process of Programming

When you say something to yourself, either positive or negative, you are potentially wiring it into your brain.

Anything you say out loud, or think silently to yourself, that expresses a feeling about you or anything else, is self-talk. Some of your self-talk may be good, and some of it may be bad. *All of it is being recorded by your brain.*

It is to the important subject of self-talk, and how to reprogram the brain in a positive way, that I have devoted most of my professional career. During the past three decades, along with the founding of the Life Coach Institute, which uses self-talk to help people create positive changes in their lives, I've written a number of books that explore the subject of self-talk in depth, and I've published many recorded self-talk programs covering a variety of personal growth subjects. Self-talk has been at the center of the seminars, lectures, and training workshops I've conducted around the world.

In the field of personal growth, self-talk has been a relevant topic for many years, but today, self-talk has become more relevant and more important than ever. That's because of the discovery that neuroplasticity and the neuroscience of self-talk are intrinsically tied to one another.

Key Point:
Our self-talk is the primary source of the new programs our brains wire into place.

It is our self-talk, good or bad, that the brain hears most. And it is our self-talk that ends up determining most of our successes or failures in life.

Can self-talk be that important? Yes, it can, especially when you recognize it is the prime programmer telling our brains what programs to wire in. It is the one message-giver that never stops. It is our self-talk that forms our beliefs, sets up our personalities, and determines who we become.

If you received only one message approximately every 45 seconds from your own self-talk (you receive many more than that), and you're awake 16 hours a day, your self-talk is telling your brain what to wire in next, non-stop, *more than a thousand self-talk messages a day.* And in your brain, every one of those messages gets recorded.

To make the important subject of self-talk clear, it will help to identify the two distinct and very different forms of self-talk:

1. NEGATIVE SELF-TALK (harmful)

This is the most common form of self-talk. It is self-talk of the negative, random, usually unconscious kind, in its often casual, yet always harmful form. This is the negative self-conversation that goes on in the minds of all of us until we learn to eliminate it from our lives.

Negative self-talk is a part of the noise we talked about in the previous chapter—the noise our brain plays randomly for us as we go through our everyday lives. It is the negative, self-doubting kind of self-talk which is the result of the programs of negative self-worth or negative beliefs about ourselves that we have wired into our brains in the past.

It is negative self-talk we are experiencing when we say such things as:

"I can't remember names." "I'll never amount to much." "I never have enough time." "I'm just not creative." "I already know it won't work." "I just don't have the patience for that." "With my luck, I don't have a chance." "I lose weight, but then I gain it right back again." "I'm no good at math." "I can already feel my memory slipping." "I can't do anything right." "I never know what to say." "When will I ever learn!" "I'm too shy." "I just can't seem to get anything done." "Nobody likes me." "I don't have the energy I used to." "I'll never get it right." "I never get a break." "What's the use?" etc., etc., etc.

Even more important to our sense of long-term self-identity and value, negative self-talk causes that same kind of self-deprecation to become wired into *all* of the attitudes and beliefs we have about ourselves.

And furthermore, negative self-talk also invades the attitudes and beliefs we have about everything *else* in our lives. That's why the glass becomes half empty instead of half full.

145

It's based on the number of neurological programs that become wired into the brain, to see the glass that way.

As a result, negative self-talk can pervade, degrade, and diminish every positive trait we have. It can reduce us to believing we are a lesser person, somehow of lesser quality, and cause us to believe we live a life of less importance than someone else—while at the same time it casts a shadow of doubt and negativity on what we experience in the world around us.

This is especially unfortunate, since that entire process—that "reality"—takes place only in the gray and white matter of the brain of each individual, and in actual fact, may have *nothing* to do with the *real* reality.

Such diminishment of the individual's self-image, as an example, is the product of inaccurate thoughts which were repeated often enough (negative self-talk) that they were wired into the brain as "facts," and the brain believed them to be *true*. They're not "facts"—and, in this case, what the brain believes to be true, *isn't true*. It's just *bad wiring*.

That's what negative self-talk does. Until we learn better, we all use it, and some people use a lot of it. Negative self-talk has no helpful place in our lives, and it should be gotten rid of entirely.

Key Point:

Negative self-talk, and the way it wires the brain in a negative way, creates the difference between people who find success and happiness in life, and people who do not.

If you know people who are very negative, keep in mind that *they weren't born that way*. (Remember the infants in the newborn nursery?) If they're extremely negative now, as adults, they got programmed that way, first by other people, and then by themselves, through their own self-talk. They didn't try to become that way; it's their programming.

2. POSITIVE SELF-TALK (helpful)

"Positive self-talk" is the supportive, high-quality, healthy, consciously self-directed form of self-talk. It is the process of sending specially-worded messages to ourselves, to actively wire specific, positive neural pathways in the brain.

As we're discussing it here, positive self-talk is something we practice and learn. Positive self-talk is not an accident we can just hope for. Once you're grown, it doesn't come by accident. If you want to rewire your brain in the right way, learning it is a must.

It is positive self-talk we're experiencing when we imprint our brain with messages like:

"I am in control of every thought I think, and everything I do." "My day is up to me, and I choose to make today an incredible day." "I choose to have a great attitude, and it shows, today especially!" "When I have a problem, I deal with it, I overcome it, and I learn because of it." "I always choose the path that is the healthiest and the best. I make good choices." "I can do this, and I know I can." "I feel great! My mind is sharp and clear. I'm organized and in control." "I do everything I need to do, when I need to do it." "I choose to believe in myself—today, and every day." "I'm on top, in tune, in touch, and going for it!"

Positive self-talk is vitally important to each of us. In fact, without it, even a little of it, we would find it difficult to live, or to move forward in life. Positive self-talk is instrumental to what happens to each of us next. While both kinds of self-talk, negative and positive, wire our brains with images of ourselves and the world we perceive, it is this second, *conscious* form of positive self-talk that we use by choice, and always in the most healthy and beneficial way possible.

Positive self-talk is not only conscious on our part; it is also *mindful,* it is *focused,* and it is *intentional.* It is the most energetic level of healthy self-direction we use. This kind of conscious, positive self-talk is used and practiced by the most aware and successful people.

This is the form of self-talk that turns lives around, changes self-doubt to self-belief, replaces fear with determination and strength, gives individuals the fortitude to move mountains of adversity in their lives, and literally gives back to people the promise and potential they were born with in the first place.

The Right Self-Talk is Never "Pollyanna Positive." The Right Self-Talk is Always Practical.

Using positive self-talk is not an expression of naiveté, ignoring problems, or living a mindset of an unthinking person who is only "Pollyanna Positive." Positive self-talk addresses the problems of life, and deals with each of them. But while being realistic, it addresses those problems with an attitude of the expectation of optimal achievement, rather than with a belief that success is doubtful, or failure is likely.

When they first hear about positive self-talk, before they fully understand it, some people believe that those who think in a positive way cannot possibly be realistic. From their point of view, *life is full of problems,* and *that's* what we should be focusing on. They think anything else is fanciful and unrealistic. "Life is tough," they say, "and you should just get used to it." And to them, *that's* being practical. They don't understand that their brain is actually following the programs that are wired into it most. When you focus most often on the problems and difficulties in life, that darker picture of existence is exactly what your brain will recognize most, seek most, *and create more of.*

People who learn to use the right kind of self-talk are not avoiding problems that need tending to. But by being positively proactive and focusing on *solutions* in a positive, purposeful way, they deal with problems more quickly, get past them, and move on to something else.

To be successful over time, you have to wire your brain for success. People who wire their brains to dwell on problems, and fail to recognize the positive possibilities of life, wire their brains for failure.

Planning Your Programming

Positive self-talk is made up of self-directed messages that we *choose.* (I know many successful people who, each morning, *choose* to have a totally successful day. I have never met anyone who got up in the morning and said, *"Today I choose to have the worst day of my life."*)

The right self-talk is the kind of wiring you can program by design. And you can make sure the self-talk you use contains the correct word-for-word instructions your brain needs for the best results.

Those are the precise messages you *should* be wiring in to the autopilot directing your *present* life now, in order to move it more in the direction of your positive *future*.

It is this self-talk we use to make each day better and more in our control. But more importantly, it is also this form of self-talk that becomes the actual program directions we give to the brain when we want to create long-term program changes.

What are You Really Wiring into Your Brain?

Earlier, I gave you a few examples of negative self-talk, and also a few examples of what positive self-talk sounds like. The first example of negative self-talk on the list was *"I can't remember names."*

Keep in mind that when you say *anything* to your brain, it will immediately search for and review every *other* program you have already wired in that is a similar kind of program. As a hypothetical example, let's take that simple, seemingly harmless, negative self-talk statement, and show you what saying just that *one* message may actually wire into your brain.

What you said:
"I can't remember names."
What your brain recorded:
"I can't remember names. I have the world's worst memory. I'm always embarrassed about that when I meet someone. I wish I were smarter, but I'm not. Oh

well, some people are just smarter than me. Better-looking, too. Why didn't I get the brains my brother got? I'm not good at meeting people. They probably look at me and think, 'What an idiot.' No wonder I'm not better at meeting new people. I'll bet they don't even like me. Why should they? I know I'm overweight. Oh well, what's new? I always forget people's names. I'll bet my boss noticed. How embarrassing. That's just me. Oh, well, tomorrow's another day. I won't be able to remember names then, either."

Imagine recording all of the above in your brain, and telling your brain to wire you that way, *permanently!*

What happened is that your brain is so smart and so fast that instead of just listening to the simple statement of negative self-talk you gave it (*"I can't remember names"*), like a tenacious reporter for a tabloid newspaper, your brain pulled up every *similar* (equally negative) thought or program you had on file.

Your brain then instantly reviewed those similar programs, compared them, and re-imprinted every one of them that had anything to do with how well you do, or don't do. This holds true not only in remembering names, but in any social circumstance you're in, how smart you may or may not be, how you think, and dozens, hundreds of programs *that were emotionally connected to,* but went far beyond your original, seemingly innocent thought.

That's why negative self-talk is so harmful. It not only wires your brain with the thought of the moment; it *reinforces* every *other* program you have stored that agrees with the negative nature of your "momentary," "unimportant," "unnoticed" negative thought. And each time you think it, it happens again!

Now let's say you had chosen instead to wire your brain with something of a positive nature—something that would *help* you instead of working against you. So let's say that the next time you have the opportunity to be introduced to someone new, you *consciously* change your self-talk. This time, instead of repeating the old name-forgetting program once again, and saying *"I can't remember names,"* you give your brain an entirely new and different message.

This time, what you say to your brain is:

"I'm really good at remembering names."

What your brain records when you say that:

"I'm really good at remembering names. I'm interested in people, and it shows. I have a great memory, especially when it comes to meeting new people, remembering people, and always remembering their names. Anytime I meet someone new, I choose to put 100% of my focus on them. I notice their appearance, the clothes they're wearing, whether they're smiling or not, how they're feeling, why I'm meeting them, and something interesting and memorable about them. When I'm interested in others, they're more interested in me, and it shows. I remember people. And I remember their names."

That's what your brain will record, *assuming you have those kinds of programs stored in your neural networks*, so they can be called up at a time like this.

If this is the first time you're using this positive form of self-talk, you may not immediately remember the name of every new person you meet. It can take a while. (Remember, you are rewiring your brain.) But what do you suppose will happen if you *always* use the right self-talk, in that, and in every area of your life, every chance you get? It should not surprise you if you end up doing incredibly well!

The key to changing your self-talk is repetition, repetition, repetition. Whether you're listening to recorded self-talk sessions or practicing it daily on your own, the programs in the brain that are wired in most strongly, and most often, always end up being the programs that win.

Not every one of those new programs will immediately change your life or create a new success. But the more you *build them*, the more they will begin to *build you* and create your success. When you build new programs, you are building the *you* that you have chosen to become.

Self-Talk and Neuroplasticity

The concept of self-talk is more relevant today than ever, because of the discovery of neuroplasticity, and the important role that these two concepts play together. They rely on each other.

Self-talk is one of the most important "managers" of your neuroplasticity. That is, you direct your brain with self-talk emotionally, mentally (intellectually), and in every other way, as long as you choose to do so. *It is your mind and your self-talk that feeds and teaches your brain.*

153

And when it comes to your "mind," it is the messages you have fed to your brain (and wired in) that will end up inhabiting and becoming the mind you think with.

Before the discovery of neuroplasticity, many people thought our self-talk was no more than our own internal conversation with ourselves—usually random, unconnected thoughts, with no effect on our brain chemistry. We now know that view was not only inaccurate, it was dangerous.

Of all of the ways we get programmed, it is our self-talk that plays the single most important role in the programming of the brain. If you have the wrong self-talk, your life will be a struggle, and cannot work well. If you use the right self-talk, you will wire your brain in the best possible way—and the results will show in your life.

Positive self-talk is you talking to your brain, repeatedly giving it precise messages of clear direction, telling it what you want to do, moment by moment, day by day. Your self-talk puts you in charge of your thoughts, your choices, and your actions.

And while it's wiring your brain with your instructions, your self-talk—the important, self-directed kind—is setting the course of the next thoughts, motions, actions and forward steps you will take.

Self-Talk Rewires Your Brain and Your Life

As we've discussed, *all* self-talk imprints or wires your brain. The negative kind of self-talk causes you to fail. The positive kind sets your brain on a path of winning. The question, "Which kind of self-talk would you like to have working for you?" has an obvious answer.

I can't begin to number the many inspiring stories of what happens in people's lives when they learn that they can rewire themselves with the right self-talk. The words I first wrote many years ago have proved to be incredibly true: *When you change your self-talk, you change your life.*

When I began writing about and talking about self-talk on radio and television and in seminars, many people decided to try changing their self-talk, and they literally began changing their lives for the *better.* The calls and letters with their stories began pouring in, and they've never stopped.

It was because of seeing many examples like those below that I was encouraged to continue exploring self-talk and what it could do for people.

As one example, I received a hand-written letter on school notebook paper. The letter was from a boy named Billy who wrote to tell me he'd had a lot of problems, he had no dad at home, and he'd gotten involved in a gang, and with drugs.

One day, as an experiment, Billy's teacher began playing self-talk I had sent to her, on a tape player in the classroom during study period. She played the self-talk out loud in the classroom every day for several weeks.

In his letter, Billy wrote that as a result of hearing that self-talk every day, he had started to look at himself differently than he had ever seen himself before. He had never heard anything that positive and encouraging in his home. He wrote that because of the self-talk, he had left the gang, had gotten off of drugs, and had begun to turn his life around. Beneath his name at the bottom of the letter, he wrote his age. Billy was just 16 years old.

Another teen, a young girl I'll call Kendra, was starting to have problems and get into serious trouble because of low self-confidence and low self-esteem after moving to a new neighborhood and changing schools. As she told me, "Whatever there was out there to be doing, I was doing it." The situation became so bad that Kendra was staying out all night, and when she was at home, she had closed off to the point that she refused to even speak to her mother and her other family members.

One day Kendra began overhearing her mother playing recorded self-talk in the background over breakfast in the kitchen. The self-talk the mother was listening to included such phrases as *"I'm on top, in tune, in touch, and going for it."*

That self-talk wasn't being deliberately played for Kendra; it was being played to help Kendra's mother change her own self-talk and programs, and she played it every morning. But Kendra was also hearing it each day when she came out of her room for breakfast—and over time, the self-talk began to have the same positive effect on Kendra as it was having on her mother. In fact, they actually started to listen together each morning.

The problems didn't go away overnight, but after a few weeks, Kendra's attitude and behavior started to change. She began communicating with her mother again, with both of them working together to repair the damage done to Kendra's life from all the wrong, toxic programs she had gotten from negative influences from the world around her and a poor choice of friends.

Eventually, repeated listening to the self-talk not only helped Kendra change to a healthier new lifestyle, choose more positive friends, and essentially get her *life* back, but it also gave her the self-esteem and the confidence to enter a teen beauty contest—and Kendra won!

When the young teen was crossing the stage to accept her crown, she searched for her mother's face in the crowd, smiled proudly, and mouthed the words, clearly and directly to her mother, *"I'm on top, in tune, in touch, and going for it!"* The phrase she used to celebrate her success contained some of the exact words of self-talk Kendra and her mother had listened to together over breakfast each morning. The picture they painted in advance had become Kendra's new reality.

I'll never forget a woman named Millie, who came up to me during a break in a seminar I was conducting on self-talk. As the slight, erect woman held my hands tightly, her eyes full of tears, Millie related how, when her husband had died, she could barely go on living. She told me she began using self-talk every day to help her cope with the painful loneliness and the loss of her husband. She said that because of the self-talk, she had found a renewed life of hope and belief in herself and in her future once again. She had come to the seminar just to let me know. Millie's tears were happy tears.

It's Never Too Late to Change

I received a letter from an elderly priest, who I'll call Father Brown. He was a man of wisdom who had counseled members of his church for many years. Father Brown told me that after reading one of my books on self-talk, he was deeply

157

saddened because the information about self-talk had not yet been available long ago when he first began counseling.

One line from the priest's letter stood out so strongly in my mind that I decided to call him. His words were, "Think of how much time I've wasted." He wrote that he could have helped so many more people, as he put it, *". . . if only I had known."*

I called him long distance by phone that evening, and talked with him. He sounded very sad, as he spoke of all the missed opportunities to help others heal their minds along with their spirit.

I asked him, "Father Brown, how old are you now?"

"I'm 80," he answered.

My next question was, "How many years of counseling time would you say you have left on this earth?"

"Maybe five or six years," he answered.

We talked for a time about his love for his work and the people in his ministry, and then I asked him this: "Father Brown, how many people do you think you could help with self-talk, starting *now?*"

There was a pause, and I could hear the smile in his voice when he answered. "I don't know, Shad, but I can't wait to find out!"

By the end of the call, Father Brown was excited about the future. He was already planning ahead, and was enthusiastic about the ways that adding self-talk to his current counseling ministry could help the people he cared about most.

A man who had been severely depressed, who had lost his wife, his family, and his job, wrote to tell me about the night he was alone in his living room, holding a revolver in his hand—ready to end his life. The television happened to be on in the background, and his attention was caught by a program I was on.

I was talking about how you can change your old mental programs, no matter how bad they might be. He heard me say that if you change your self-talk, you can get new programs—and, in time, a new life.

The man wrote that what he overheard from the television at precisely that time was enough to get him to stop for a moment. He decided to put off ending his life *until he watched the rest of the television program.* So he sat on the sofa, laid the gun down beside him, and watched the rest of the show.

By the time he wrote to me, he had been busy working at turning his life around. It had taken work, but with his new mindset, he had gotten his job back, he had gotten his wife and family back, and he had gotten his life back. And he was very much alive!

The Right Self-Talk Makes the Difference

I want to be very clear on this next point. I don't mean to imply that all the people in these stories had to do was listen to self-talk, and their lives magically got better. In each case, it took real time and diligent effort to make the necessary changes. But it was the self-talk that, in each case, made the critical difference between success and failure.

I relate these life events because they, and many others like them, so strongly got my attention. But it was the rest of the life stories that also convinced me of the power of self-talk. They were the stories of everyday people using it to change their everyday lives.

People were losing weight, getting their finances in order, getting more organized and in control of their lives, going back to school, overcoming problems in relationships, and achieving many other things in their lives they had never thought possible or had struggled with in the past. And they were doing all these things by changing their self-talk. They were literally rewiring their own futures.

Recently, I received a web posting from Liz, a woman who had hosted a training seminar on self-talk I conducted. Liz had been sharing self-talk with her seven-year-old daughter, Laura. The daughter had been listening to a self-talk recording I created called "Self-Esteem for Kids." That particular self-talk is recorded in the cartoon-like, animated voice of a character called "Shadrack the Self-Talk Bear."

In those recordings, Shadrack plays a game with his young listeners called "Repeat After Me." By listening and playing the game, kids learn word-for-word self-talk that teaches them the kind of positive attitudes that stay with them for a lifetime.

The mom told me her daughter was listening to Shadrack the Bear and his positive self-talk the night before Laura had to perform in a gymnastics competition. The child did very well, and the next day Laura said to her mother, "Momma . . . I think Shadrack lives in my head!"

How helpful it would be if every parent understood that we can change what lives in our kids' heads! What a lifelong gift we could give to our children, if we always took the time to put the right messages into their young and eagerly-awaiting minds!

160

Throughout the time I've seen self-talk work so successfully in people's lives, most of the stories have been of people who used the idea of self-talk to reach greater heights, achieve higher goals, and choose to move from "good" to "really good," or to "great."

The simple, straight-forward concept of changing a person's self-talk from the "average," unconscious, and often negative kind, to the better, more positive kind of mental self-direction, has created untold improvements and achievements in people's lives. I don't know how many millions of dollars have turned to wealth and income for the people who applied this one concept of managing their lives by managing their thoughts.

But the truth of what the right self-talk can contribute to a person's life does not begin or end with dollars or wealth. That truth lives in the daily habits of people who choose to achieve their best; it empowers their most creative and inspired dreams, and it moves them upward in the direction of their greatest opportunities.

Chapter 18

Using Self-Talk in Your Everyday Life

Because of neuroplasticity, changing your self-talk clearly works, and it makes life-changing differences in people's lives. But just as important are the smaller changes, the little things that add up, day after day. That's where changing your self-talk—rewiring your brain to the positive—has its most profound impact.

Here's how self-talk and neuroplasticity work together in everyday life.

Let's say Jennifer really wanted to lose weight and keep it off. She knew her self-esteem was low, and she wanted to change it. Lately she hadn't liked herself, and she didn't like how she looked.

After failing with one diet after another, Jennifer finally decided to change the negative programs she had about herself, and to replace them with a healthier mental picture of herself. Instead of trying another unsuccessfully diet, she decided to change her self-talk—and that's what she did.

When Jennifer changed her self-talk, she changed her programming. By doing that, she actually changed the wiring of her brain. Jennifer wasn't dwelling on the rewiring that was going on in her brain, but she felt different, and she felt a lot better. She was creating a new picture of herself, and with her new self-talk, she was learning to value herself more highly.

Because of that new picture of herself in her mind, Jennifer began to "become" the new picture of herself that her new self-talk had created. And *that's* what got rid of the unwanted weight. This time it was a "different" Jennifer that was taking the weight off.

The key point here is that before Jennifer changed her self-talk, she had been fighting the *symptoms* of the problem instead of fixing the problem itself: in this case, years of negative self-talk that had destroyed Jennifer's picture of herself. By changing her self-talk, she wired new circuits into place; the old negative programs were eliminated—and so was the extra weight Jennifer had been trying to lose.

Self-talk and neuroplasticity work together to create actual changes in something as important and essential as self-esteem (and weight-loss). It requires the choice to do it, and there are rules to follow, but anyone who wants to use self-talk to change things in his or her everyday life can do so.

Applying self-talk to ordinary life experience shows that the choice to change your *input* will change the results you get. That makes perfect sense, of course. What you wire into your brain will *always* determine what you get back out.

Taking a Walk through "Self-Talk Park"

The brain creates new neural pathways as a result of repeated input. When the carefully worded phrases of self-

163

talk are listened to often, when they're played out loud from a recording, or when they're repeated consciously and mindfully, the brain imprints those messages in neural pathways. This process either creates new pathways (with new messages) or reinforces and strengthens the pathways of messages which were previously imprinted.

To illustrate how this works, we'll visit a place I call *Self-Talk Park*.

Imagine you have just been born, and you find yourself magically standing in a beautiful park with lush green grass, some trees, and a blue sky overhead with a few fluffy cumulus clouds. It is a perfect park and a perfect place to be as you begin to grow and learn. There are no pathways or walkways (it's a new park), just endless expanses of soft green grass, and some trees.

Then let's say you get a "message." Someone says something to you, and your brain is recording the message for the first time. As you get the message, you find you can walk a short way through Self-Talk Park. When you look behind you, you can't even see where you walked. You haven't formed a path or walkway yet, because it is the first time you walked this way.

Then you get the same message again. So once again you walk the same way, retracing your steps, but when you look back, you still can't see a path. The message is still too new, because you've walked this way only twice.

Let's say you get that same message again, and then another time, and then a few more times, and in time you receive the same message over and over, each time retracing your steps along the same path.

Now, when you look back, you can see the beginning of a pathway being formed. And each time that same message is repeated, you walk over the same pathway, and each time you do, that same pathway becomes clearer and stronger.

In the brain, every time the same message or the same thought or the same experience is *repeated*, the brain sends nutrition and energy to that neural pathway, and the pathway gets stronger. In your own Self-Talk Park, as you received those repeated messages, you walked those same paths over and over again, with each repetition making the paths clearer and stronger. (That's how repeated messages form neuron pathways in the brain.)

As you grew older, your Self-Talk Park, once green and pristine, with no pathways at all, started to get filled up with a pathway for this and a pathway for that. In time, some of those pathways, because of more repetition, became walkways. And then, through even more repetition, some of those walkways became small roads, and then larger roads. As you grew older, some of them became even larger; they became highways.

By the time you were grown, your Self-Talk Park was a map of many thousands of paths, roads, and highways. Some of those paths, through repeated use, became superhighways—strong, clear power roads you used day after day—and eventually you didn't even have to think about it. You could, and would, automatically take the easiest road to follow.

This is why you can get up, get dressed, and go through your day, giving little or no thought to the routine actions involved. Activities that once required a choice or a decision, you now follow according to the choices and decisions you

165

made a long time ago, when you first caused those neural pathways to be created. Now those activities are automatic, because you've formed neural pathways that direct each of them (like the autopilot we discussed earlier).

If you could post a huge, wall-sized map of your own Self-Talk Park on the largest wall in your home, by the time you reached adulthood, the picture of your once beautiful, untouched park would look like a chaotic, busy road map with hundreds or thousands of clear, strong roads and highways leading in every conceivable direction. Some of those roads would take you where you want to go. Some of them would lead you in the wrong direction, or they would lead you nowhere, with nothing but uncertainty at the end of the road.

When you look at your wall-sized map that is now filled with roads and highways, what you're looking at is the sum total of your programs. You're seeing your *beliefs*, your *attitudes*, your *opinions*, and all of your *habits*—all of which were formed by repetition, and all of which are now physical neural pathways in your brain. What you're seeing is "you"—and *why* you do almost everything you do.

The Pathways You're Following Now

Whose footprints, traces, tracks, or trails are you following in your own Self-Talk Park? Unless the pathways are good ones and you want to get more like them from the same positive sources, it may not even be important where you got them.

Because your future can be changed based on the new pathways you choose to create, *where* the older negative tracks came from is no longer the important issue. The ones that count are the pathways you place in your brain and in your life starting now, and choose to follow.

Counselors and life coaches who understand this, help their clients focus on the future—not on a past that may have let them down. The field of positive psychology is made up of counselors and therapists who encourage their clients to also look *forward* instead of only revisiting the problems of the past. (Each time you revisit and reimagine the hurtful things in your past, you repeat them, and therefore, once again, you *rewire them*.)

If you have a problem from the past that you need to look at in order to understand it, and wire it differently, do that. With the help of a competent counselor, you can make sense of the situation, reframe it, rewire it, and put it to rest. But then, do your best to let the past experience go. It's the neural pathways you wire in *next* that will determine where you will go next.

Your Neural Pathways Direct Your Life

As we grow and learn, we come to believe that our own pathways, our own roads, are the best roads to follow—often regardless of whether they're really leading us in the best direction. Those roads become our beliefs about everything.

Unfortunately, many of the roads that were created for us, or that we created through our own negative self-talk, were not "true" at all. They only got there because our brain

167

created them for us, day after day, input after input, belief after belief. It made no difference what was really *true*, and what *wasn't* true.

Those were the messages we received. Those were the pathways we walked again and again. And in time, our entire identity, our "self," was created by the paths we walked most.

In time, each of us began to believe that the picture we had of our own identity was cast in stone. We believed we could make little changes, but when it came to changing the big things—our personality, our intelligence, our happiness set point, and so on, we believed making those kinds of changes was physiologically impossible. We believed they were unchangeable, because we just weren't "cut out" for those kinds of changes. We looked at life as though our mental road map was an accurate picture of who we really were, and for the most part, that was how things would stay.

Our beliefs, our prejudices, our opinions, our thoughts, and our actions all gathered together to create a composite picture of who we believed ourselves to be. We knew we could improve ourselves in some ways—that's what "personal growth" was all about—but we believed we were still cutting the "new" person from the same cloth the "old" person was cut from.

The science of self-talk shows us how we can take charge of our own positive programming—our "reshaping." (We can virtually "change the cloth" from which the new person is being shaped.)

When I first wrote about self-talk, before the concept of neuroplasticity had become known, those of us who were studying the mind in this new way understood that self-talk was changing the brain. But it took more scientific research, and finally the ability to watch brains actually grow new neurons and new networks of connections, to prove to the rest of the world that our thoughts themselves were literally rewiring our brains.

Finally, we could watch our thoughts, and we learned that not only were our brains busily rewiring new circuits for us, they would also imprint and wire the circuits *we wanted them to put in place.* We were making our own self-talk highways. We were watching our brains change themselves—and they were doing so by *our choice,* under *our direction.*

It's not hard to figure out that if a person's negative mental programs, created in large part by their habitual self-talk, were being recorded in their brain and acted on as though they were true, that person would literally create his or her own problems.

It's equally clear that if you can replace negative or unhealthy mental programs with a whole new language of positive self-talk, and know that those new programs are being recorded in your brain and acted on, your chances of success at anything you attempt will be vastly improved.

Self-Talk and "Affirmations"

The terms "self-talk" and "affirmations" are sometimes used, incorrectly, as synonyms for one another, but they're not the same.

Affirmations do "affirm." But in today's context, affirmations are positive statements which are most often used in spiritually or holistically oriented forms of self-expression, such as, *"I am at peace, and one with the divine universe."* Or, *"I am guided to seek and find the most positive outcome in all things that I do."* Those can be good affirmations, but the self-talk used to direct your own programming each day, when you take control of your brain's neuroplastic imprinting, has to be more specific than that.

When you're actively involved in changing neural pathways in your brain, your self-talk should be precise, direct, clear, and to the point: *"I get things done. I take action. I set clear, specific goals. I work at them. And I reach them."* Those kinds of targeted directions tell your brain exactly what to do and how to do it, and in your brain, they create specific, directed results.

The self-talk that says, *"I get up at 6:15 each morning,"* is not an affirmation in the spiritual sense. It is a precise directive to your brain, telling it exactly what you choose to do, like the pilot of an airplane programming precise directions into the airplane's onboard computer. (Airline flight officers never type "affirmations" into the airplane's navigational system. They type *directions*.)

Affirmations tend to create a softer, more general spiritual environment of the mind. If you've been using and practicing affirmations, you may want to keep doing that, but add clear, specific, directional self-talk, so your brain knows *exactly* what you want it to do next

Why We Use Self-Talk in the "Present Tense"

When you read or listen to any well-constructed self-talk, you'll find it is written in the present tense. For example, let's say you set a goal to spend 30 minutes a day improving yourself.

If you were to use self-talk that says, *"I'm going to spend 30 minutes a day improving myself,"* what message would that actually give to your brain? It would say "I'm *'going'* to . . ." which says, *"later,"* or *"some other time,"* or, *"when I get around to it."*

When you put your self-talk in the present tense, it becomes a specific direction for your brain to take action on *now*.

"I spend a minimum of 30 minutes each day improving myself."

If you want to lose weight, instead of saying, *"I'm going to lose 15 pounds,"* give your brain a completed picture of what you want to accomplish: *"I choose to weigh 110 slim, trim, healthy, attractive pounds."* That's the picture your brain will see, and that's the slim, trim, healthy, attractive you that your brain will help you create. You're saying, *"This is the me I choose to be. This is the me I want you to create. Here's the exact picture of what I want you to do."*

Regardless of the area of your life you want to work on and program your brain to wire in—your health, attitude, relationships, finances, family, career, etc.—you are the engineer who is giving the completed design to the road-builders. Putting the picture of what you want in clearly-worded present tense gives your brain a completed picture it can clearly see and immediately act upon.

Chapter 19

How to Use Positive Self-Talk to Rewire Your Brain

Your self-talk is the most important player in directing your brain's neuroplasticity to create the pathways you choose to help you run your life.

Do you have any programs right now you'd like to change? Do any of your programs ever work against you? Do you have any programs from your past that create a self-image of you that doesn't live up to you as you'd like to be now?

It's been my experience that *all* of us have programs we'd like to change or get rid of. In fact, when they learn about self-talk and programming, most people are more than anxious to trade in their faulty programs for new ones—if they could just figure out how to do it.

Since the concept of self-talk has grown dramatically in public awareness, there are now advice-oriented articles and blogs on the subject—usually under a heading that reads something like, "Is your negative self-talk hurting you?" or "Make sure you have the right self-talk."

Those articles are pointing in the right direction. If the authors miss anything, it's the specific steps their readers need to take to make the actual changes in their self-talk. (Just deciding you're going to change your self-talk, starting tomorrow, doesn't do it.) One headline read, "If you're using negative self-talk, *stop doing it*." That may be good advice, but you have to know what to do next.

The Steps That Work

Years of study and experience in this field have shown that there are four key steps to changing your self-talk. If you have programs you'd like to change, start with these four steps:

1. *Monitor.*

Listen to your own self-talk. Monitor everything you say, anytime you speak. Listen to what you say when you're in a good mood; listen to what you say when you're in a bad mood. Monitor what you say during the first minutes of your morning. Listen to yourself during the day, and at the end of your day. Listen to what you say when you're with your friends, and listen to yourself when you're alone.

Listening to your own self-talk is part of mindfulness; your own self-talk is something you should be aware of at all times. To learn what your own programs really look like, monitor what you say out loud, but also monitor what you say or think silently to yourself. (In self-talk, your *thoughts* are as powerful as your spoken words.)

173

Listen to everything you say or think—whether it's directed to yourself or to someone else—but pay special attention to anything you say to yourself about *you* or your own life that could work against you. Pay *particularly* careful attention to negative self-talk statements like those we looked at earlier:

"I'm not that smart;" "I could never be good at that;" "Nothing ever goes right for me;" "It's no use;" "Another blue Monday;" "I'll go, but I know I'm not going to have a good time;" "Everything I eat goes right to my hips;" "I'm not going to get my hopes up;" "I always get sick this time every year;" "It'll never work;" "That's just my luck," etc., etc., etc.

When you begin to listen carefully to your own self-talk—including everything you think—you don't have to analyze where those programs came from or how you got them. The purpose of this step is simply to be completely aware of what your self-talk is *now*.

That will give you a picture of the programs you have that are unconsciously managing your life for you. It will help you recognize some of the programs you want to change.

If you hear your own self-talk sounding down, negative, doubtful, or less than positively in control of your own life, those are programs you will want to replace.

Begin to Notice the Self-Talk of Others

When you're listening to your own self-talk, also begin to listen to the self-talk of other people in your life. It can be very revealing. Almost without exception, the people with the best self-talk will also be the people who are doing best at life—not just financially and socially, but *emotionally*. Those with better self-talk are generally people who are happier, more productive, have a better attitude, and are going for it.

2. *Edit.*

Even though your self-talk is a heavily-programmed habit, and you may not usually be aware of it, you have the power within you to change what you're going to say or think next.

Any time you're about to say anything you don't want to imprint and record in your brain, stop right there. Don't say it. Don't *think* it. *Replace it.* Think the opposite. Think the *best*, not the *worst*. Reframe the thought. Rewrite the script. What you say or think next *will* be recorded in your brain. If you don't want your brain to record it, think something else, something positive that works for you instead of against you.

Change *"I can't possibly do this,"* to *"I can do this, and I know I can."*

Change *"This is difficult,"* to *"I can make this work."*

Change *"They never listen to me,"* to *"They love to hear what I have to say."*

Change *"I'm so stupid,"* to *"I'm smart, I have a great mind, and I know how to use it."*

175

Change *"I hate this weather; it's raining,"* to *"Somebody needs the rain, and it's a beautiful day for me in every way."*

Change *"I'll never be able to fit into these jeans,"* to *"Every day I'm reaching my goal of weighing the weight I choose."*

Change *"My kids will be the death of me yet,"* to *"My kids are my life."*

Change *"I'm in a rut and I can't get out,"* to *"I'm in charge of what I think next, do next, and achieve next."*

Change *"The only photographs I take are bad photographs,"* to *"I love taking pictures!"*

When you edit your words and your thoughts from the negative to the positive, you're not kidding yourself, you're not lying to yourself, and you're not ignoring reality. After all, your negative self-talk was not true the first time you used it (and started imprinting those false programs into your mental computer), but you never wondered if you were lying to yourself, then.

At the moment you first make the change, the new direction will not yet be wired in, so it might sound like that's not *you,* or it's not true. But what you're doing is giving new messages to your brain—messages your brain will record and act on. What your brain records repeatedly is what your brain will do. *That's* the new reality your brain will create, and that *will be you.*

Editing, by itself, will not rid your brain of the negative programs you have already recorded and stored. But editing what you think and say will help keep you from getting more of the same. (And you could end up taking *great* photographs.)

3. *Practice Being Your "Inner Counselor."*

I first discussed this concept in the book *What to Say When You Talk to Your Self*, and I have seen it help many people make important changes in their lives. One reason I personally like the idea of self-conversation, or the *inner counselor*, is because it's so practical—it brings *cognitive common sense* into the picture.

Here's how it works. You have talked yourself *into* many of the programs you now have, so when you want to change them, it would make sense that you could also talk yourself *out* of them, by reasoning with yourself. With an understanding of the right words to use, and with some practice, learning to use this tool can lead to positive changes in your attitudes and beliefs about yourself.

This step calls for you to consciously take on the role of your higher, more enlightened self, and to practice counseling your *everyday self* from the position of a wiser, less emotionally involved *inner counselor*. It asks you to consciously replace fear and false notions with reason and reality.

When you first begin to practice this step, your old programs—and the emotions attached to them—will still be in control. They are habits. But with consistent repetition of the right new messages, the old programs will begin to give way. Because of the repetition, the old programs are being replaced by *new* neural pathways and connections you're consciously creating in your brain.

177

Learning to be your *inner counselor* is not designed to replace a professional counselor or therapist. Seeking professional support and guidance from a positive-oriented and future-directed counselor or therapist can be very helpful. In fact, an increasing number of counselors are helping their clients develop and practice many of the tools we're discussing here.

Improving Your Day and Rewiring Your Brain

In actual practice, becoming your inner counselor works like this: As an example, let's say Paul has a recurring attitude that is negative—something that has been with him since adolescence. Paul's teenage years were difficult, and programs of not measuring up, which were wired into him then, have stayed with him.

Now Paul is in his mid-30s, and he knows enough about neuroplasticity to realize that his persistent lack of self-confidence could be changed if he were to begin having a new kind of conversation with himself. He's coaching a Little League team, and he enjoys it, but every time his team has had a bad day, he has felt like he's a failure who has just let everyone down.

But now, when he feels the emotions that signal his self-doubt are coming to the surface, instead of hiding from that feeling or trying to ignore it until it passes, he consciously steps into his new role as his inner counselor and creates a completely new dialogue with himself. It might sound something like this:

"Okay, Paul, the game hasn't gone well, but that's okay. What you're feeling really has nothing to do with this game, anyway. It has to do with you losing belief in yourself when you were in Little League when you were 14. That was a long time ago. It's over. And it wasn't as important as you thought it was. You got past it, and here you are, a coach! Let's make today a great day, no matter how the game comes out. All your kids are winners, and you are, too. Let's show them your best."

You'll notice that in this example, Paul's self-dialogue is in second person—*"you"* instead of *"I."* Paul is using second person because he's talking to himself from the position of a higher self—the part of him that he imagines residing above, or outside of, himself. This higher self is more objective; it doesn't register the same emotions Paul is feeling inside, because the wiser Paul is consciously detached.

(Some people are more comfortable talking to themselves in the more familiar first person as *"I."* Both forms work.)

If Paul continues to keep his inner counselor close by, and repeats a similar scenario each time the problem comes up, he will, in fact, be rewiring his brain with new circuits that let him know the fear and doubt he felt as a fourteen-year-old are no longer real—they come only from past programs that are no longer valid.

The key to the success of the inner counselor is that it gives you a way to create new neural pathways by using cognitive tools like fact, intellect, and logic—exactly the kind of tools our emotions so often ignore. While it's true that emotions themselves chemically increase the strength of programs, in this case it is the repeated self-dialogue that allows thoughtful *reasoning* to create the new pathways.

Because this form of cognitive inner dialogue can play a valuable role in managing positive neuroplasticity, I would encourage you to practice taking on the role of your inner counselor. In other words, when you have old programs that consistently work against you, like a habit you'd like to change, talk to yourself.

Finding the more objective, wiser part of your awareness can take practice, but you'll find it's worth it the first time you observe yourself literally talking the old "you" out of an impending road rage, stopping an argument before it starts, seeing a new goal in an unlimited new way, or adjusting your attitude up a notch even though you just got yelled at by your boss.

In each case, you are rewiring or replacing circuits in your brain that are not valid. They have persisted simply because until now they have never been recognized for what they are and dealt with in a way that would change them.

The goal of this step is to practice—through frequent repetition—playing the inner counselor so naturally that you begin to do it without having to remind yourself. The result will be a constant rewiring of some of your most important neural pathways—from problem, to solution, to getting on with your life.

4. *Listen to Self-Talk.*

Today, thanks to science and neuroplasticity, the best way to wire in new programs is by listening to self-talk. Listening to the *right* kind of new self-talk makes sense; it was by listening to the *wrong* kind of self-talk that we got most of our negative programs in the first place.

I first began experimenting with recording early forms of positive self-talk in the 1970s, before I wrote the first of several books on the subject. It became clear to me early on that the new kind of self-talk I was working with had to follow specific programming rules if it was to work effectively.

The question was, "How can any individual practice self-talk with enough repetition that it will form new neural pathways in the brain?"

Because I had studied foreign languages, and at one time was a Spanish/English interpreter, I believed that if people were able to listen to specially recorded self-talk programs—exactly as if they were learning a new language, by listening to it—it would be possible to learn self-talk with enough *repetition* to actually wire the new programs into their brains.

Just reading the words of self-talk, or repeating them to oneself occasionally, would not create sufficient repetition. But being able to listen to the new self-talk for 15 or 20 minutes a day would create the repetition necessary for the new programs to become wired in.

Because the goal was to rewire the brain in virtually any area of a person's life (relationships, self-esteem, health and fitness, career, etc.), the new self-talk I was writing and recording had to meet important requirements that would help the brain wire in the new messages, no matter how serious the problem was (how entrenched the old negative programs were.)

I also learned it wasn't just the repetition of the self-talk itself that made it work. It was *how* each self-talk phrase was repeated that would help the brain imprint it and store it permanently.

181

This is why, when you listen to a recorded session of self-talk today, each phrase is repeated three times, and is spoken each time with different intonation and emphasis. This specific process creates more neuronal connections in the brain, wires more neural networks, and links the self-talk messages to other similar programs in the brain.

In addition, because of what I'd learned about writing self-talk, it had become clear that the "imagery" of the self-talk was very important. Every word and every phrase was significant, not only because of the wording of the message itself, but because of the mental imagery it would create and wire into the brain of the person who was listening to it. Listening to self-talk *is* learning a new language, word for word (this time it's the language of self-belief, success, etc.), but it's also imprinting positive new *visual images* in your brain at the same time.

Recorded self-talk comes in the form of individual program "sessions" on specific subject areas—things you want to work on in your own life. This allows you to hear, each day, a new "background" to your life that is made up of positive messages about you that are being wired into your brain as new "truths about you."

The recorded self-talk sessions started out on cassettes, and then progressed to CDs and downloads. Self-talk programs are now streamed directly to phones, tablets, or any listening device. (You can try this out for yourself at www.selftalkplus.com.)

Each recorded session lasts from about 10 to 12 minutes for kids, to about 18 to 22 minutes for adults. The length of each self-talk session is based on "attention learning span," which gives us the highest level of retention in the shortest frame of time. (Attention learning span is shorter with kids, and longer with adults.)

The self-talk you listen to is not subliminal, and it's not hypnosis. It is specially-worded self-talk messages that, with repetition, train your brain to override, replace and erase negative programs. You hear the new self-talk clearly, your brain records it, and through repetition, you create new neural pathways in your brain *based on the number of times you listen.*

While you're listening, your brain is automatically searching for any other similar programs you have already stored, and begins to wire those earlier programs together with the *new* self-talk messages, combining them and creating new, positive superhighways in your brain.

Listening to self-talk is a combination of the science of self-talk and the brain's neuroplasticity working together to change your programs.

When and How to Listen to Self-Talk

There are a few rules to follow when you listen to self-talk, that will help you get the best results:

1. *For the first few days, play the new self-talk "in the background."*

We learned to speak our first language by having it spoken in the background, from the time we were born to about the age of three. We didn't attend a single class to learn our first language. And *most* of the words, sentences and phrases we learned were not even being spoken to *us*. They

183

were just there, spoken by others in the *background of our lives.* But our brains were listening, recording, imprinting and wiring in those words, sentences and phrases perfectly—or at least as perfectly as the people around us were speaking them.

Now, when you begin listening to recorded self-talk, treat it like learning a positive new language, and play it in the background. Your brain will be listening, whether "you" are or not.

2. Listen to self-talk while you're doing something else.

Listen to self-talk while you're getting ready in the morning, exercising, driving in the car, eating dinner, checking your email, doing something around the house, or almost any other daily activity.

Listening this way does two things.

First, while your brain is initially getting used to the new self-talk, your old programs won't argue with it as much. This is because you're just letting the new self-talk play "passively" in the background, and not focusing too much attention on it. (You'll be focusing on it more later, after you've become familiar with the new messages you're getting.)

Second, playing self-talk in the background helps alert your brain that the self-talk you're learning is a natural part of your day. Instead of it being an "exercise" set apart from other activity, it becomes a natural part of your everyday life.

3. Listen first thing in the morning, anytime during the day, and just before you go to sleep at night.

184

You can listen to self-talk anytime, but listening first thing in the morning is a great way to start the day. (A 10-minute argument in the morning can dump enough toxic levels of chemicals into your system that it takes the next 8 *hours* for you just to get back to normal. Imagine hearing, instead, 15 or 20 minutes of the right kind of positive *self-talk* at the beginning of each day.) Start the day by listening. It will start your day off on the right track, your attitude will reflect the self-talk you're listening to, and you'll feel the positive effects throughout the day.

During the day, people listen while they're driving in the car, at work (often with earbuds), working around their homes, while they're eating, or almost anytime at all.

One of the best times to listen is while you're doing any kind of exercise, like while you're walking or running. (Healthy *body*, healthy *mind*.) For many people, hearing the positive self-talk also makes their workouts seem easier and go faster.

Also, listen to self-talk just before an important meeting, or anytime you have to be extremely alert and on top of your game. While it continues to work at wiring the positive new programs into your brain, self-talk also "fine-tunes" your brain to deal with the moment in a better way.

At night, just before you go to sleep, is another good time to listen. If you listen to the right program of self-talk at that time, you'll be more relaxed, your mind will be calmed by the self-talk, and your brain will continue to work on its new programs while you sleep.

4. *Focus.*

After you get used to listening to self-talk played in the background, begin to focus to a greater degree on what you're hearing, and give it more conscious attention.

If you do nothing more than let the self-talk play in the background, your brain will record it, and it will work for you. But when you begin to give it more focus, your brain will pay greater attention to it, and the programs you're listening to each day will become stronger.

(To stream specially-recorded self-talk programs to your phone, tablet, or listening device, visit the Self-Talk Institute's membership site at www.selftalkplus.com.)

Chapter 20

Neuroplasticity with an Attitude

Attitude plays a powerful role in our success as individuals. When it comes to powers of the mind, other than *belief* itself, if you could change just one thing about someone that would guarantee a difference in that person's life, it would be his or her *attitude*.

Our attitude is the face we show to the world around us, but it's also the emotional measure of the self we feel inside. Attitudes are both emotional and intellectual; we can "feel" them, and we can also think within them to manage them.

Our attitudes are mercurial; they can be dark and foreboding one moment, and bright and uplifting the next. Bad news often creates bad attitudes, and good news can create good ones. Attitudes make or break days, start us or stop us, keep us going, hold us back, or kick us into high gear.

The father of American psychology, William James, said, *"The greatest discovery of my generation is that human beings can alter their lives by altering their attitudes of mind."* A hundred years later, it is one of the greatest discoveries of *our* generation that we

187

now know the mechanism by which we can create and control our attitudes by our own choice.

Which Comes First—Your Programs or Your Attitude?

This brings us back to the *"neural activity feedback loop"* we discussed earlier. Your attitude changes the wiring in your brain. Then, in turn, your wiring affects your attitude, which in turn rewires your brain again, which, in turn, affects your attitude . . . and so on.

Let's say that on one day you find yourself with an attitude that's "down." It's not a chronic form of chemical depression, but it feels just as dark. You're filled with gloom, and nothing looks bright or even remotely happy or promising. Even the smallest problem seems overwhelming. You look at yourself in the mirror, and an unhappy face stares back at you. You spend your day in this dark mood, unable to get rid of it; the weight of the feeling is just too heavy to shake off.

But then, while you're in the depths of this mood, the telephone rings. You answer it, and on the other end of the unexpected call is the most important person in your life, with the best news you could ever have hoped for. And like the sun suddenly breaking through the dark cloud that hangs over you, a golden ray of light shines through—and in moments, the depressing gloom lifts and is gone.

In this case, what broke the cycle started with the unexpected phone call. But the clue here is that *the depression changed with a change of mind.* It was your internal perspective

188

that changed. And it is that perspective, with or without the phone call, that is up to you. At any time you choose, you get to create the golden rays of light.

Every Negative *Thought* Attracts
Other Negative Programs

What precipitated the gloom in the first place was a gathering of old negative programs, brought together by bad news or something going wrong that day.

In the brain, negative thoughts attract other thoughts just like them. (This is called *"association,"* and is a neurological linking of similar circuits or programs.) When you have a negative thought, programs of a similarly negative nature become activated, and new connections are made in your brain, linking the negative programs together, and making them stronger. What might have been only a moment of disappointment turns into a union of dozens of negative programs that hijack your entire attitude and hold it hostage.

In our example, it was the good fortune of the phone call that summoned up equally strong, but previously dormant positive programs, chemically and electrically networked them together, gave you a burst of chemical stimulant, and immediately infused your attitude with a renewed sense of positive belief. The sunlight broke through, your face changed from a dark frown to a bright smile, and you were fine again.

The question is: What do we do if there is no phone call?

The answer is: *We make the call ourselves.*

189

At any time in the cycle, you can step in and change the cycle by choice of will. It is this amazing capability to change our own attitude that separates people of a positive mindset from people who wait in the darkness for someone to call (or something positive to happen).

The expression *"Use it or lose it"* is also appropriate when referring to creating the neural pathways that create good attitudes. It is the person who continuously upgrades his or her programs from negative to positive that has the best chance of having fewer dark moments, and the quickest turnaround back to a brighter day.

It is those who literally fill their minds with healthy experiences and the right self-talk, whose positive mental programs are ready for the call to action anytime the need for an instant attitude shift comes up. The more you *use* these positive neural pathways, the less chance you'll have of *losing* them—in fact, the stronger they'll become.

Who, then, is in control of your attitudes?

Your attitudes are entirely up to you.

All Attitudes are Habits, and All Habits are Programs

We weren't born with any of our attitudes. All of them were programs we repeated often enough for them to become wired-in habits. Over time, we built up a menu of thoroughly-practiced attitudes we could draw from anytime we wanted.

Some of our attitudes are so interwoven with specific emotions that we have a hard time telling the attitude from

190

the emotion. Anger, for instance, is an emotion, but it also becomes a practiced attitude, one we unconsciously call up anytime someone says or does something that's not to our liking, and we're too busy or too tired to deal with the problem in a rational way. We *become* angry. We may not even realize we're doing it. But it's an easy attitude to put on, we're used to doing it, and it seems so *normal.* (Anger management problems are almost always based on programs that need to be rewired.)

The problem is, negative attitudes like anger are so easy to adopt that we can do so without thinking about it—and once again, our not-so-bright negative programs take over, without our stopping for a moment, thinking about it, recognizing that this is ridiculous, and taking mindful control of our lives once again.

Attitudes that are *"negative," "jealous," "thoughtless," "greedy," "self-pitying," "despairing," "hopeless," "bitter," "vengeful," "resentful" "gloomy," "haughty," "dramatic," "argumentative," "sarcastic," "closed-minded," "uppity," "controlling,"* or *"bullying"* stand out clearly when they're displayed by someone else. But when we take on one of those roles ourselves, we may not even know we've fallen into a negative attitude—and when we do, we're not only hurting ourselves, we're hurting others around us.

All of these attitudes are "roles." None of them was actually real until we took on the character and brought it to life—characters made up of nothing more than neural networks in our brain, that someone else or our own negative self-talk put there in the first place.

We're Not Born with Our Attitudes— We Learn Them

With enough repetition, attitudes can become "personalities." A strong attitude, practiced over time, creates so many neural networks and connections in the brain that it takes on a life of its own—and the person literally becomes the personality of the attitude.

As just one example, I've observed people who, when discussing some trait they have—for example, talking too loudly, being argumentative or frequently interrupting others—will sometimes say, *"That's just the way I am."* In saying that, they superficially find themselves blameless for the discomfort they're causing everyone around them.

But it *isn't* just the way they are. Not really. They weren't *born* talking too loudly, being argumentative, or interrupting others; they learned and imprinted those traits (usually from people close to them) often enough to wire in powerful, unconscious programs, and they're not even aware it's not who they really are at all. It's just who their programs have caused them to become.

The good news is that because the problem of insensitive, negative programs was caused by the neuroplastic wiring of that person's brain, the same neuroplasticity can also rewire them *out* of the problem.

To do that, what's required is that they become aware of the insensitive attitude, and through repetition of the right new programs, trade in the old attitude for a new one. The answer will be to consciously choose to adopt the new attitude, and repetition, repetition, repetition. (As yet, there is no safe, healthy pill to fix talking too loudly, being argumentative, or frequently interrupting others. If there were, I suspect it would become a best-seller.)

Choose Tomorrow's Attitude the Night Before

It's a powerful idea to choose the attitude you're going to have the next day, before you go to sleep the night before. That idea works because we have a choice—and we would never fall asleep thinking, *"I choose to have a bad day and a terrible attitude tomorrow. Goodnight."*

Tonight, just before you go to sleep, take a few moments and choose the attitude you're going to wake up with in the morning, and the attitude you choose to have throughout the day tomorrow. Be very specific. *"I choose to wake up tomorrow morning with a positive, optimistic, go-for-it attitude. That's the attitude I choose to have all day."*

Repeat that several times just before you go to sleep, or write it down and read it just before you close your eyes. And then, first thing when you wake up in the morning, begin the day by saying, *"Today I choose to have a positive, optimistic, go-for-it attitude. That's the attitude I choose to have all day."*

When you do that, not only will you be clear and mindful of your programs, you will almost certainly have a better day.

Do the same thing again tomorrow night, and then again the next morning. Write the self-talk statement that describes the attitude you would most like to have, and read and repeat it several times each night and morning.

Only a few years ago, this idea would be thought of as a self-help technique that only devoted personal growth enthusiasts were apt to try. Today we see it differently. We

193

now know that with every repetition of those few simple words each night and morning, you're actually laying out the construction lines for a new highway you're beginning to build, then clearing the ground, preparing the base, and paving the roadway.

Day after day, repetition after repetition, you're forming a strong new neural network in your brain, and you're constructing that road with your mind. It is a physical, chemical and electrical highway that is really there, in your physical brain, getting stronger, connecting with other similar highways, creating a mindset you will soon awaken to each morning—and it sets the direction for the day ahead.

Who's Choosing Your Attitude Today?

Along with your conscious self-talk, your attitudes not only play the strongest role in directing your behavior each day, they are also the #1 manager of the unconscious side of your brain's neuroplastic programming process. At the same moment, your attitudes are outwardly shaping your day, while they are inwardly managing your neural programming—your wiring.

When you're in the middle of your day, and you find your attitude is starting to slip downwards (maybe things aren't going too well at the moment), stop for a second and ask yourself, *"Who's directing my attitude right now?"*

Anytime is the perfect time for your inner counselor to step in and state the choice you wish to make for the attitude you'd like to have: *"Listen up! Time for an attitude change. Time for 'gratitude and serenity.'"*

194

Canadian psychologist Donald Hebb's famous saying that *"neurons that fire together, wire together"* explains how this works. If each time a problem comes up, you choose a new, more positive and productive attitude, *you will, in time, wire that new, better attitude to that old problem*, and in so doing, you will change your brain from its old *"problem orientation"* to a new *"solution orientation."* Eventually, when a problem comes up, you'll already have a "solution path" wired directly to the problem.

An Attitude with a Purpose

As I mentioned previously, we recognize the power of music to create an instant change in our mood. The right music can literally change our day.

This is because music bypasses our analytical mind and comes directly in through the door marked "emotions, feelings, moods, and memories." We don't have to think about it—we just let the music take us to that place in our minds that makes us feel uplifted, or better, or serene, or romantic, or whatever else we'd like our minds to help us feel.

Music is also safe; it turns on powerful chemical switches in the brain, but music itself isn't a drug, so it has no negative side effects. And music is accessible. With portable electronic music players, we can listen to anything we want, almost anytime we want.

Having loved music of every kind for as long as I can remember, I found when I first began writing years ago that I wrote better while listening to certain kinds of music.

I began to experiment, and soon found that the mood of the *words* I was writing was directly reflecting the mood of the particular piece of music I was listening to. When I wrote my first book, I wrote all of it to a short list of very specific musical selections I sought out, music I found would bring out the right emotion or the right kind of expression in whatever I was writing at the moment.

I did this faithfully throughout the time I worked on my manuscript. At the end of each writing day, I paused the music at that point. When I sat down to continue writing again the next day, I continued playing the same piece of music I had been listening to, at the exact point I'd paused it—and continued writing on the same paragraph I was working on the night before.

Because of the music, I was able to move my writing seamlessly from the night before to the next day, as though I had not stopped writing at all in between. I literally "set up" the right *attitude*, and the attitude set up my thoughts. Now, nearly 30 years later, when I re-read the pages I wrote at the time, I hear that music. And no matter where I am when I hear that music, I can see those pages.

What I did was to wire the "emotional music imprinting neurons" in my brain to the "logical writing imprinting neurons." As a result, those neurons organized and connected themselves *together* as I constructed that set of neural pathways in my brain.

I used music as a tool to create an attitude with a purpose—a *writing attitude*—one I knew would elevate me to the proper emotional level for the writing, as well as help to guide my sentence construction, logic, and focus each time I sat down to write. The moment I heard that specific music, my mind moved into my "writing attitude," and I would type the next words of the book. To this day, 16 books later, I still follow that practice.

Create the Attitude to Get the Job Done

Although we don't always take something like listening to music so seriously that we consciously try to build a neural network in the brain to create an attitude around it, the same process is happening in our lives every day—*unconsciously.*

Recall the statement that neurons that fire together, wire together. It tells us that when we connect two or more inputs to the brain in a significant way (think "my first kiss") the brain forms a stronger neural network as a result.

That would suggest that your best—or strongest—attitudes will be those that have a wealth of imagery or repeated experience connected to them. This is why, instead of trying to create a "success attitude" just by demanding of yourself that you think or feel "successful," you're encouraged to *visualize,* and to put success-oriented pictures on a "vision board" on the wall, and focus on those pictures every day.

When someone wants to build an attitude of success in sports, like running, for example, they will practice self-talk which focuses on performance and endurance, as well as thoughts and images of winning—and they will burn those pictures into their mind for days or weeks *prior to the event.* When the day of the event arrives, that's the attitude that will already be set up to take them to the finish line.

(In one research study of two groups of cyclists, the group that practiced positive self-talk for 2 weeks prior to the

197

test and during the test itself, had an *18% higher endurance time* than the cyclists who did not practice self-talk.)

Your Attitude Starts with Your Self-Talk

The easiest way to create a change in your attitude is to use the right self-talk to set it up. Many people listen to recorded self-talk to do that. Or, at times, even a single phrase of the right self-talk can set up an attitude.

For each of the attitudes we will look at here, I've included an example of written self-talk that will bring that attitude into mindful focus.

When you read this form of self-talk, or repeat it to yourself, you're giving specific instructions to your brain. You're saying, *"This is what I want my attitude to be. Go to work on it!"*

When you give your brain specific instructions, it will put its powerful programming processes into action, and help you accomplish what you tell it you want it to do.

Once you've selected the attitude you want to have, you can begin by consciously practicing both the self-talk and the attitude throughout the day. The more you practice doing this, the more it will begin to become a *programmed attitude* you can call on at any time.

Remember, because your neurons are firing and wiring together, each day you practice having a certain positive attitude, and that day produces positive results, *your brain will be wiring that attitude to the positive results it is creating.*

Chapter 21

The "Top 12 Positive Attitudes" to Wire In

M any people take their attitudes for granted, or don't recognize they can have control over them, if they choose to do so. At any time, you can *choose* one or more of the attitudes that will help you the most.

But it will help if, like the cyclists who practiced self-talk, you first make sure, with *repeated practice*, that you're wiring them into your brain.

Your attitudes are tools with which you both direct yourself *internally* and affect your life *externally*. Healthy, positive attitudes help you succeed. Unhealthy, negative, or harmful attitudes make life difficult and help you fail. It's not the best idea to take any of your attitudes for granted, or just hope for the best. The goal is to be able to have any healthy, positive attitude you'd like to have, the moment you want to have it.

Of the many attitudes you might choose, here's my list of 12 attitudes that will help you the most. (I have this list posted on the wall in my studio.) The more you practice using each of these attitudes, the more your brain will wire them

199

into place. Practice them enough, and you'll have them for life.

You will likely have other attitudes that come to mind, that would also be helpful. Add those to the list.

(You'll notice that on this list, there is no one attitude entitled "Love." That's because, in my experience, that one element, *love,* should live within and throughout *all* of our most positive attitudes, and in a perfect world, underlie all of them.)

Here's the list:

1. An Attitude of *Optimism*

This attitude begins with self-talk that says, *"I am up, positive, optimistic, and going for it!"*

Optimism is just plain *healthy!* We now know that statement is scientifically correct, and the relationship between your optimism and your health, well-being, and success in general is undeniable.

When you practice an attitude of *optimism,* you win more in life in every way, you feel better doing it, and you get healthier in your mind and your body. When you practice believing in the *best,* you're actually directing your brain to biologically affect your cells in a positive way. You are also bringing up stored mental programs that help you look for more options for interacting with the world around you, and help you discover more positive possibilities.

A long-term attitude of optimism is a habit. It becomes a "wired-in" part of who you are, based on the number of times you practice having it.

2. An Attitude of *Peace and Serenity*

To create this attitude, begin with self-talk that says, *"I choose to live a life of peace and serenity. Right now, this moment, I choose to be calm and serene, and I feel the quiet contentment of peace and well-being within me."*

As you repeat this self-talk, take a deep breath, slowly, and hear the words in your mind. As you take another deep, relaxing breath, let a feeling of quiet calm come over you. Let any cares or worries fall from your shoulders and drift away. Feel the spirit within you lift up, as you nod in the affirmative, and welcome the loving comfort of peace and tranquility. You are, right now, creating the soothing touch of serenity. As you're creating the feeling, you're rewiring your brain.

When you frequently repeat this soothing exercise, you'll be "permanently" wiring a new program into place. You'll be building a new neural network in your brain with the words *"Peace and Serenity"* written above it. That's a great attitude to have any time you need it—and it can become a wonderful new component of your personality.

When you read the information on meditation that we'll be discussing in a later chapter, you'll see it is also helpful to combine meditation with practicing an attitude of peace and serenity. The two go together.

3. An Attitude of *Kindness and Harmony*

Self-talk: *"I care about others, and today I choose to express kindness and harmony in my life."*

How can you *not* have an attitude of kindness and harmony? Isn't that *life?* But to a lot of people, because of their programs, kindness and harmony is *not* life—at least, it is not *their* life. They were raised (programmed) to think differently, that the world is tough and competitive. They were taught the meaning of life is to *"look out for number one."*

The opposite of that set of neural programs is to grow up believing people are good, people count, and life is not just about self-protection; life is about loving others, being kind and caring, and making things *work.*

You choose the path. The more you walk it, the more your brain will record it. The more your brain records it, the more those programs will determine your beliefs. And the more you believe it, the more you will walk that path, in a positive cycle that can change any attitude for the better.

If you aren't already practicing this attitude, it would be interesting to watch what happens if you test living this attitude for even a single month. When we practice an attitude of love, kindness and harmony, it's astonishing how *other* people around us begin to change.

4. An Attitude of *Determination and Focus*

This attitude is born from self-talk that says, *"I am determined to reach my goal. I focus on my goal, I work at it, and I make it happen."*

When you move through a typical day, ask yourself this: before you even think about it, what is the physical position of your shoulders, what is the level of your chin, how tall do you stand, what is the stance of your feet, and how clear is the focus in your eyes? (Our physical posture almost always reflects the posture of our attitude.)

If your day needs special determination and focus (read also as, *"strength and attention"*), you can set up an attitude to do that for you.

If you have an obstacle to overcome or a challenge to meet, consciously adopt the attitude of *determination and focus.* Give your brain the clear instructions: *"I am determined to reach my goal. I focus on my goal, I work at it, and I make it happen!"* When you need it, you'll be amazed at what this one attitude can do for you.

5. An Attitude of *Intuition and Awareness*

Self-talk: *"Today I choose to be clear and sharp, and tuned in to everything within me and around me. I am in touch with my intuition and my feelings, and I listen to the messages they give me."*

When you have an important decision to make, or when you're trying to understand or sense something, it helps to call on that intuitive part of yourself that "knows."

There is a part of us which is exceedingly wise, that knows more than we are consciously aware of. There are many ways to tap into that wisdom. This attitude will help. Practicing an attitude of *intuition and awareness* will alert your spirit and your senses to the task. This is "mindfulness" at

203

one of its highest levels, and is another area that will benefit from practicing meditation.

Even if this is an idea that is new to you, try it for yourself. Practice having an "awareness" that is beyond your ordinary thoughts. Listen to you innermost feelings, the almost silent nudges that wait just beyond the level of your everyday senses. Ask the questions in your mind, and wait for the answers. If you ask, the answers will come.

6. An Attitude of *Spiritual Well-Being*

Self-talk: *"I choose to fill my life with unlimited spirit, and I feel its uplifting energy in everything I think and do."*

If you're a person of faith, your attitude probably already shows it. Not everyone who has a strong sense of the spiritual dimension of life shows it publicly—but you can express it internally, with your self-talk, and with your attitude of mind.

If you live a life that is spiritually connected, you don't have to be told what to do with that. But keep in mind that your attitudes wire your brain—so the more you practice having an attitude of spiritual well-being and enlightenment, the more spiritual you will feel and become. Your brain is designed to help you in every way it can. Helping you live more spiritually is one of the things it will do.

Even if you haven't been an especially spiritually-oriented person, I would suggest you consider actively practicing a spiritual attitude. That's because the most successful, self-fulfilled, and *happiest* people I have ever found, always report that an important part of their balance as an individual comes from the spiritual side of their life.

Whether, to you, the word "spirit" refers to a higher power—something greater than ourselves—or simply that special energy and enthusiasm you feel on a particularly great day, the benefits to you from focusing on this one aspect of your life can be immeasurable.

Even if all you do is to conscientiously practice imagining, for three or four weeks, that there is a greater part of you that you can't see, that "spirit" part of you will empower you to do better, and will help you create greater outcomes in your life each day.

If you were to test practicing one month of programming your brain with an attitude of *spiritual well-being*, and one month entirely without it, I would not be at all surprised if you chose to continue the attitude that includes spirit.

7. An Attitude of *Service to Others*

Self-talk: *"I choose to live my life each day, mindful of my service to others. I know that my value as a person is measured by the good I am able to do."*

The attitude that asks, *"How may I help you?"* or *"How may I serve you?"* is one our world could use more of. That attitude leads to the question, *"How can I help someone other than myself in some positive way today?"*

Service to others is a key ingredient to creating success in almost anything you do. But even more compelling is the link between helping others and living a quality life. Choosing an attitude of service can turn an average day into a winning day, for you as the one who helps, and for the person who benefits from your caring. And repeating that kind of win-win attitude day after day rewires your brain in the positive, forms the habit of helping, creates emotional healthiness, and changes your life for the better.

8. An Attitude of *Thankfulness*

Self-talk: *"Today I choose to be thankful for all the good in my life. I am so fortunate to live the life I live, and right now is a good time to say 'Thank you.'"*

It's hard to imagine a day in which we could not write a long *list* of things to be thankful for. But in the rush of life, that list can remain forgotten for days or months on end, or until, here in the United States, the Thanksgiving holidays roll around and we dutifully recite the list of things we are thankful for over a turkey dinner.

The *Attitude of Thankfulness* is a perfect "replacement" attitude. Our mothers told us this—that we should be thankful for what we have, instead of being upset about what we don't have.

When you're feeling down about almost anything, *read your list* of the good you have in your life. When you get angry, *read your list*. When you're worried or uncertain about the future, *read your list*. When you're having a bad day, *read your list*. When you miss out on something, or didn't cross the finish line in first place, *read your list*. Your life will get better.

Mentally reading your list of what you're thankful for, makes you feel more appreciative and better at the moment. It also wires gratitude into your life, makes you more mindful of recognizing the blessings that surround you, and focuses your programming on the positive rather than on the negative.

So this is an attitude that creates all-around positive programming. When you were a child and you complained about something, and your mother told you to be thankful for what you've got, she was right.

9. An Attitude of *Forgiveness*

Self-talk: *"I choose to forgive . . . all others, and also myself. No matter what, I choose to forgive, and move on with my life."*

It's not surprising that so many therapists have had to work hard to help their patients get rid of guilt. Guilt, out of place, can be one of the most damaging of all human emotions.

It's one thing to feel remorse and attempt to correct the wrong; it is another to allow guilt to consume and destroy one's self. That's because other than the recognition of the wrong and the choice to change and make amends, the ongoing emotion of guilt has no positive value in the life of the individual.

(When you blame someone else for something they've said or done, it's quite possible you should actually be blaming their programs. The person is responsible, of course. But if they had gotten different programs, they probably wouldn't have done whatever it is you're blaming them for. The same is true of you.)

Adopting an *Attitude of Forgiveness* gives you the opportunity to confront guilt, forgive others and yourself, and get on with your life.

Make amends if things need mending, but don't allow the guilt itself to program your brain with endless remorse. That helps no one, and hurts you and your future. Forgive everyone else. Forgive yourself. Then move past it. That's an incredibly healthy attitude, and a wonderful program to wire into your brain.

10. An Attitude of *Healthiness*

Self-talk: *"I choose to live my life today, and every day, in a healthy, positive way—physically, mentally, emotionally and spiritually. I choose to be healthy."*

This attitude needs no explanation, and there is no excuse not to adopt it and use it often. When it comes to *healthiness,* we know it, we understand it, we can choose it, and when we're mindful of it, we live out more of it.

Healthiness is one of the clearest and most dramatic examples of the power of programming. You do things like eat, sleep, exercise, and practice moderation entirely based on your wired-in personal health programs. Most of your healthiness is the result of your habits. All of your habits are the result of the programs you have wired into your brain.

An attitude of positive healthiness affects what time we get up in the morning, impacts the habits and the friends we choose, helps us set and reach long-term health and fitness goals, and puts the spring in our step. And it goes beyond that—into our mental focus, our peace of mind, our spirit, and the joy we have in living successfully each day.

11. An Attitude of *Patience*

Self-talk: *"I choose to create calm, quiet patience in my life each day. When I do, I also remove stress, and add to my well-being and peace of mind."*

The reason people joke about not having patience so often, is because so few people have enough of it. When you think of someone with unending patience, the easiest picture to bring to mind is either an elderly person, or someone who lives in a monastery.

Patience seems to be a common virtue that is always in short supply. And yet patience is *essential* to any well-made plan, and is vital to attaining any measure of peace and serenity.

I've found three certain ways to master this one, and to have enough patience to spare.

a. Practice having a broad perspective.

One way to cultivate patience is to develop a perspective on life that is above, outside of, and far beyond your normal day-to-day existence, the kind of perspective you might have in a spiritual state of mind. This is a perspective that allows you to view life from an elevated level, less affected by a day-to-day, short-term view of life.

One reason I so often choose to write near the water when I'm working on a book is because of the freeing perspective that the endless sea, and waves on a shoreline, can give.

When you're facing the water with nothing in view that was made by man, you're seeing the exact same scene some other human, just like you, saw long before you—perhaps thousands of years ago. And someone else just like you will probably be standing on that same shore, seeing that same scene you're seeing now, a thousand years after you're gone. To me, that very long view of reality creates valuable perspective

I know that choosing to have a long-term perspective on life, and actually *living* that perspective, are two very different things. That's because we have so many attention-grabbing mental programs that are immediate, demanding, and not long-term at all.

A few of the best ways to help you overcome *short-term* programs when you need to create *long-term* perspectives, are *1)* consciously choosing to think long-term, *2)* practicing daily meditation with a focus on creating a longer-term picture of life, *3)* reading history, and *4)* reading the biographies of people who lived at least a century ago. (When we read about their lives, we realize our own problems can seem like nothing compared to theirs, and we often gain a better perspective and insight into our own lives.)

b. Live a long life—or think like someone who has.

Another way to develop patience is to wait until you have lived for many years. Older, wiser people seem to master this one just by the fact that it took so many years to get there, that their view of life is longer than ours—and one of the results of that view of life is more patience.

c. Practice having an "attitude" of patience.

The third way I'll suggest here, to master having patience—and by far the easiest to do—is to practice having an *attitude* of patience, and *wiring it into place in your brain.*

Doing this may take some time, but it's definitely worth it to your sense of well-being, your peace of mind, and your general sanity. And the good news is that you end up creating a more patient attitude *while you're practicing having it.*

This doesn't mean you can't be aggressive or assertive when you need to be. It just means you may want to wire yourself with the empowering habit of patience, since without it, aggression and assertiveness are no more than exclamation points without a sentence.

Try being exceptionally, wisely mature and patient for 24 hours. Throughout the entire day, practice being patient— about everything. Then do the same thing the next day, and the next, and so on. When you do that, you will begin to wire your brain with some of the most intelligent habits (and positive personality traits) you can ever acquire.

12. An Attitude of *Success*

Self-talk: *"I choose to succeed in my life in every way. I was born to be successful, and that's how I choose to be."*

211

The most important element that separates people who succeed from people who don't is their choice to do so. *Nothing* replaces an *attitude* of success.

The reason this one concept, success, is so hard for so many people to really "get," is that "success" in life is not a single program in the brain; it is *many* mental programs that all work together to create an overarching belief. And that is the belief that changes everything.

We're not referring here to making mistakes, or experiencing failures and learning from them—this is about success overall.

Let's say you choose to have an attitude of success. What's exciting about this attitude is that when you first adopt it, your brain doesn't care whether you believe it or not. It will still wire it in! In time, when you add *belief* to the mix, the program will get stronger—but *you don't have to be successful to start being successful.*

To begin with, there is an important truth that many people are never taught: *"Success" is a group of programs.* (In this case, it is usually a lot of smaller neural networks that have wired themselves together in your brain.)

Key Point:

"Success" is not a single program in the brain. Success is made up of many neural programs that your thoughts and beliefs wire together, and aim in one direction.

Success is a series of connected programs you have to wire into your brain so completely that your brain will begin to seek successful outcomes in any circumstance, unconsciously and naturally.

This is why some people can't imagine being truly successful—while other people, with the right wiring, can't imagine failing. People who have never gotten strong, positive success programs from their parents, from the world around them, or from themselves, actually believe they are destined to be less successful than someone else. Their belief isn't *true*, of course. It just becomes true for them, because that's the only "success programs" they got.

I recognize that if you want to try this attitude on any given day, you might not feel at first that it's a perfect fit. But stay with it. The doubt you feel is just your *old* brain trying to counter the *new* message of success with old programs that tell you you're nothing special. The old programs are wrong.

But you get to replace them, and eliminate their control over your life. By changing your self-talk and your attitude, you can get rid of them. You're about to rewire your brain in a positive new way. And with repetition, you will win.

There's Nothing Negative on the List

We would never knowingly *choose* a bad attitude. So why, then, would we ever let a single negative attitude dominate our thinking for even a *minute*—let alone hours or days at a time?

Though I'm not suggesting you wait weeks or months to practice each of the 12 attitudes I've suggested here, if you did take an entire month to practice each of them one at a time, without any doubt at the end of a year you would have an amazing attitude.

In actual practice, when you work on wiring in the 12 attitudes on this list, you can begin right now to practice any of them, or more than one of them, on any given day. You'll replace negatives with positives, day in and day out, and your life will show it, beginning almost immediately.

Because of the power of neuroplasticity, your *super attitudes* will become imprinted in your brain. Those new attitudes will direct and influence every thought you think, everything you say, and everything you do every day. That's how you get better tomorrow—by practicing your attitudes today, and every day. The more you do that, the more natural those attitudes will become.

In a short time, instead of focusing on one attitude or another, all of them will begin to come together in one powerful, overall attitude of winning in life. And then your winning frame of mind will be a neurological part of you— and it will be *wired in*.

Here's the list of the 12 attitudes I keep on the wall in my studio:

Optimism
Peace and Serenity
Kindness and Harmony
Determination and Focus
Intuition and Awareness
Spiritual Well-Being
Service to Others
Thankfulness
Forgiveness
Healthiness
Patience
Success
Love

If you practice these attitudes every day, they will change your brain and light up your life.

Chapter 22

The Brain that Keeps You Young

We love good news, and no matter what age you are right now, the discovery of your brain's neuroplasticity is definitely good news! It is a wonderful revelation for everyone, and especially for the millions of people who would like to help their brain live in a more youthful place.

We've all been told that our later years are supposed to be the best years of our lives. But living with the old belief that our brains had no chance to do anything but eventually lose their youthful qualities and grow tired and diminished, many people haven't felt they had much to look forward to.

Our new understanding of the power of neuroplasticity is changing that dramatically. On the cover of this book is a scene of the sun rising over the earth from space—a new dawn. I chose this image because, in the world of mind and brain, we are experiencing a new dawn.

We now know that no matter how old you are, you can start looking forward to a more youthful, more vital brain keeping you thinking younger again, with more of the sharpness, alertness, and mental energy many scientists once believed was a gift given only to the young.

As I've said, I long believed those scientists were wrong. Twenty-some years ago I wrote a book entitled *"Finding the Fountain of Youth Inside Yourself."* In that book, I supported the position that the brain did not have to become a victim of ever-slowing vitality and debilitating aging, at least not to the degree that was commonly thought.

I would wait 20 more years before neuroscience popularized a new kind of thinking. Fortunately, it has. And what the neuroscientists have discovered not only proved the point, it's even better than we had imagined.

If you think it's too late to start making your brain feel young again—let me reassure you, *it's never too late to get better.* Your brain is still very much alive, and getting ready for your next bright idea. Even if you're getting older in years chronologically (we all are), there's so much you can do to stay younger in your mind.

One of my favorite words is the word "wonderful." As I use the word, it means *"full of wonder."* And that describes a youthful, growing, learning mind at its best. That description should apply to you.

It describes not only those individuals who are youthful in years, but those who are *mentally* youthful regardless of their age—those who choose to never let go of their wonder. (Interestingly, you cannot be filled with wonder and, at the same time, feel sad, depressed, angry, or gloomy. You can't be "full of wonder" and "down" at the same time. Completely different programs. Different connections in your brain. And a different look on your face.)

No Matter What Your Age

Key Point:

It is never too early or too late to begin exercising your brain, enhancing neuroplasticity, and being more youthful in your mind, brain, and spirit.

Regardless of your age as you read this—whether you are young, middle-aged, or older—are you as focused and clear as you'd like to be? How is your memory—sharp as a tack? How is your outlook—filled with non-stop visions of promise and potential? No matter what age you are now, if you're not already doing so, it's time to begin getting your brain into shape. If you're already doing that in some ways, it's time to do even more of it.

When I was young, an elderly man I met told me that every individual should have at least eight different vocations—eight completely different interests—in a lifetime. "If you do that," he said, "you'll always be alive while you're here, and you'll never grow old."

He told me this at a time when it was popular to have only one career, some one thing you would work at throughout your life, finally retire from your work, and then grow old, with nothing genuinely new to look forward to other than retirement.

I thought at the time that the idea of living your life with a number of different interests to look forward to was a wonderful idea. I suspected that anyone who did that not only would never get bored; they would always have something new to discover—something that would make each new morning part of a new beginning.

218

That is exactly how our brains work best: always having a new interest, like a new morning, to look forward to. I have often thought how correct that man was. At the time he told me this, he was in his 80s, and he was traveling the world. I lost track of him over time, but I have no doubt that on his last day on Earth, he was still planning what he was going to do, and where he was going to go, tomorrow.

No matter what age you are right now, if you want to be the sharpest, smartest, most mentally alive person you can be—which is how you were designed to be—exercising your brain to take you there can't be an occasional pastime or a diversion. That would be like wanting to learn a new language well enough to spend time in another country, but only working at it for a few minutes every other week. Getting smarter and getting better is a progressive accomplishment. You start from where you are now, take one step at a time, and if you keep on going, you keep getting better.

In the next chapter, I will give you a number of ways to maximize the brain you have now, build entirely new neuron pathways that will help make you feel young and keep you that way, and overall, add more *life* to your life.

Chapter 23

Neuron-Building Activities

What you learn in this chapter could open doors for you that you'll never want to close, and help you create positive mental habits that will stay with you for the rest of your life. This is not about getting a few ideas to help you improve your life in some trivial way. This is about improving your life in significant and substantial ways.

I've termed the following activities *"neuron builders."* They could also be called "brain builders." Neuron builders, in this context, involve the entire process of creating new neuronal growth, and new networks of neurons being built by your conscious choice to build them—a very exciting idea!

From Work . . . to Play . . . to a Way of Life

If you were to look at a list of positive brain exercises you could begin practicing today, your first thought might be that exercising your brain looks like *work*.

When I recommend the kinds of activities that help train or retrain your brain, I recognize that one of the reasons the good ideas work is that they start by requiring effort. But don't worry; these ideas, in actual practice, almost immediately replace the idea of work with the rewards of success, of winning, of feeling better, and of doing something of value that turns into enjoyable activity. It soon becomes an exciting game you can't wait to play.

If you want to grow new neurons and wire in more brain power, here are just a few examples of the kinds of things you should consider:

Learn to play a musical instrument
Practice meditation
Always memorize your grocery list
Learn a new language
Draw a detailed house plan
Memorize the names of all of the presidents
Get good at archery
Write a journal
Learn to write with your other hand
Design a new tile pattern for the bathroom
Remember phone numbers
Read Shakespeare
Build a detailed dollhouse
Hunt with a camera
Take a college course
Practice Tai Chi
Learn drawing or painting
Join an astronomy club

Learn to juggle
Exercise
Read books on a subject you've never explored before
Memorize Pi to the 25th (or the 100th) decimal
Give talks
Learn to play tennis
Play games that are mentally challenging
Learn crocheting, knitting, or quilting
Master the Rubik's Cube
Run or cycle
Learn a new skill and then teach it to someone else
Write a book
Sculpt a horse out of clay
Drive on a completely different road to a place you've never been before

What do all of those projects or activities have in common?

Each of them will help you rewire your brain.

Each of them will inspire and pattern your brain to grow. Your list, if you think about what you *could* do, can be as long as you choose to make it. If you were given the challenge to come up with 100 activities that would help you wire your brain, what would be the three activities at the top of your list?

The suggestions I've given you here, and many other neuron builders, all work if three things are in place:

1. *That you actively participate, with highly-focused interest in the activity, over a period of time.*

222

2. *That you repeat each new learned activity frequently and regularly.*

3. *That you stay with it, and keep doing it.*

Some thought patterns, repeated often enough, will create new neuron paths in days, and others in weeks. How long it will take for you to wire your brain in positive new ways will depend in large part on how much attention you give it.

Some wiring happens rapidly. Memorizing a two-digit number, and storing it for life, can be done in a matter of minutes. Intently playing a high-action video game can change neural wiring in your brain (or your child's brain) in a matter of a few hours.

How long does it take to grow a garden? It depends on what you plant, how much nutrition and sunshine it receives, and how much attention you give it. The popular ideas on the subject, that it takes "21 days," or "30 days," or "66 days" to rewire a new program into your brain, are not the final answer.

How long it takes to wire in a new neural pathway will depend on the importance of the message, and the amount of *mindfulness, choice, intention, focus, repetition, emotion,* and *belief* that you commit to the new program.

The good news is this: When you begin to send new messages to your brain, you'll notice some changes almost immediately. Some of your first results can be very exciting. But watch what happens when you stay with it (water the garden daily) and make it an everyday goal!

As a strong note of encouragement, most people who actively work at changing their wiring, following the guidelines I've presented to you here, start to see some of the early results—especially in how they think and also in their attitudes—even in the first few days.

Whatever Your Age, Now is a Good Time to Start Using Neuron Builders

A number of years ago, when I wrote the book *Finding the Fountain of Youth Inside Yourself*, I focused on the incredible opportunity each of has, to do many exciting new things, to find life endlessly more interesting, and to keep our brains functioning at a sharper, healthier level as a result.

I have lived a life of believing in the immense value of creativity, so I've had a lot of experience in having fun by challenging my brain. But recently, I added some new personal neuron-builders to my own list.

As an example, one neuron builder I decided to tackle was to learn to write with my right hand (I'm left-handed). I had wanted to learn to play the piano, and play it well, for a long time—so I decided to add taking formal piano lessons to the list. I also decided to study the architecture of the great cathedrals of Europe, took up archery, and began practicing Tai Chi. And finally, as a demanding mental exercise, I made the choice to master the Rubik's Cube.

The reason I chose each of these particular neuron builders was that each of them requires practice and dedication, each of them offers rewards and positive gratification (you can see your progress as you work at it), and each of them is an ongoing challenge—you may do well, but you can always get closer to perfection.

224

I had never written with my right hand, and every pen stroke would be a new neural experience in my brain. Formally learning to play the piano would tie hand/finger muscle coordination to neural pathways in my brain that had previously not been formed.

I knew that learning the details of how medieval cathedrals were built would tax both my "right-brain" imagination and my "left-brain" detail and analytical thinking. Practicing Tai Chi is both a mental and physical practice that is excellent for general health as well as creating new brain cells. Getting good at archery would require physical and visual focus. Mastering the Rubik's Cube would be mentally demanding—just the thing to get new neural pathways up and running. I had not met anyone over the age of 50 or so who had mastered it easily.

Taking the Time

You might think you could be too busy to do these kinds of things. I felt that way, too. But I found that the positive experience of tackling each of the new pursuits soon began to create changes in my priorities, in order to make room for the new interests.

As an example, having already removed almost all unnecessary television viewing from my life, I did not find it hard to watch even *less* television, so I could use the freed-up time to do something more worthwhile. (Learning to play a simple tune on the piano is better for your brain than watching bad news on television.)

225

Since you're busy, prioritize your brain-stimulating time by practicing ideas and exercises that will do you the most good, or that you will enjoy most. Remember, the list of things you can do to give new life to your brain is endless.

Here are the key requirements to keep in mind when you're choosing neuroplastic neuron builders for yourself. It's not required that each of your neuron builders has all of the following qualities, but the more of these qualities each neuron builder has, the greater the chance it will work.

1. Newness.

The activity you choose should be something new to you—something you haven't done before, or haven't done in the same way. For instance, you may have danced, but have you tangoed? You may have sketched portraits, but how about the Statue of Liberty or Da Vinci's horse?

When you want to create new neurons and new pathways in your brain, choose something that requires you to learn something more than what you already know.

How much do you know about Greco-Roman architecture, the pollination of your garden plants, how to cook a completely healthy meal, or why Thomas Jefferson was important to the founding of a country? You don't have to be a seasoned veteran of discovery; you just have to be curious and interested in learning new things.

2. Concentration and focus.

When you're using a neuron builder, the greater the intensity of your concentration, the more neural activity you will create. Also, if you've been partial to what has been called left-hemisphere thinking (analytical skills), spend time living with your right-hemisphere (intuition and feeling), and vice-versa.

For example, instead of watching the plot of the film, move to another part of your brain and watch the movie while focusing on the feelings each of the actors is expressing. Watch the colors the set director chose for mood and ambience, and ask yourself how those colors make you feel.

When you do this, you're still using your analytical brain, but you're crossing over into your emotion-centered self, and that causes more new neurons to fire. Look for opportunities to think about things differently and literally see things differently. And then apply that different point of view with robust concentration and focus.

As we discussed in the earlier chapter on focus, *real* focus is not a casual event. Real focus is fine-tuning your mind to every detail of the activity, noticing everything, tuning in to the moment, and being aware of every nuance of everything that is going on around you—the picture you see, the color, the ambiance, the sounds, the texture—everything your senses send to you.

Forcing yourself to use more concentration and focus with any neuron-building activity also does one other thing that will help you grow new neurons: it makes you *think*.

3. Difficulty.

The neuron builders you choose should be reasonably difficult. They can be fun, but they shouldn't be easy.

227

Learning to instantly recognize each of the parts of Vivaldi's "Four Seasons" may not be a difficult task for some. For others, however, it will take listening to the music with more dedicated concentration as many times as it takes for their brain to record it strongly enough to recognize and remember it.

Mastering archery can be a lot of fun, especially when you're making headway, but for a lot of people, it isn't easy. When you're practicing a neuron builder, the rule is: If you don't have to really think about it as you're doing it, it isn't an active neuron builder.

The popular idea of "no pain, no gain" is not true when it comes to strengthening "muscles of the mind," but it is true that the addition of *difficulty* itself increases the effectiveness of the exercise and the strength of the neural programs you create. Choose neuron builders that are possible, but challenging.

4. Reward.

The activities you choose should have a built-in reward or value. As an example, even in the earliest days of learning to play tennis, you're rewarded every time you score, or return the ball especially well. Learning to play a musical instrument, even as a beginner, and even just for yourself, can be very satisfying. Or simply turning the activity you've chosen into a goal with a target date and hitting your target can be a reward in itself.

As in all goal-setting, actual awards you give to yourself work well. Examples of this could be an evening out, some extra time to yourself, something you wanted to buy for yourself, etc. Giving yourself rewards can make your brain-building activity more fun, and you'll be more motivated to stay with it. (Always plan the reward and know what it is in advance. The anticipation of receiving the reward increases your level of interest, as well as your motivation to stay with it, and it helps you reach the goal.)

Overall, however, when you're doing new things to increase your awareness and your brain power, it may be the feeling of accomplishment, simply as a result of doing it and staying with it, that will be your greatest reward.

5. Measurable progress.

Each of the neuron-building activities you choose should be something that allows you to measure your success, or lets you see you're making progress. Doing complicated word puzzles can stimulate neural activity, but they can also create their own "sameness," and other than completing the puzzle, you can't tell if you're making real progress.

That can mean you're maintaining or strengthening your *current* neural circuits, but you may not be building *new* ones. But if you progress from juggling two tennis balls to juggling four and then six of them with equal dexterity, that's progress. Your brain is wiring more complex circuits, and you can see the results.

6. Stimulation.

The more of your senses you involve, the more neurons you will grow. Imagine using the neuron builder of "creating a new design for your kitchen," and then imagine you focus

229

on this just as you're going to sleep at night. If you concentrate, and if your visualization skills are good, creating your new kitchen in your mind will stimulate cell growth.

But you'll create more stimulation when you make detailed drawings of the floor plan; when you force yourself to anticipate and overcome any problems in the design; when you watch and listen to instructional videos on remodeling that you've found online; when you download an App that lets you print out a 3D rendering of your plan; when you build a scale model of the completed kitchen; when you show the model to your friends and describe your plans for the construction; and finally, when you write out a detailed materials list and an itemized budget estimate for the project.

As you can immediately see, in your brain's neuronal activity, there is a huge difference between just imagining the new kitchen, and focusing your thinking about the project in an engaging and diverse variety of ways.

Even if the purpose of this exercise was only to create a higher level of activity for your brain, and not actually to remodel your kitchen, you would have achieved an important goal. Of course, if you *did*, in fact, remodel the kitchen, and did a good portion of the work yourself, you would create even more activity and stimulation—and have a beautiful new room to show for it. Beautifully enhanced kitchen, beautifully enhanced brain.

7. Uniqueness.

Look for things that are unusual and out of the ordinary (for you). The more *unusual* the activity is for you, the more neurons and circuits will be involved and will grow as a result.

This is different from the "newness" requirement we discussed earlier. If you chose to read a new book to build new neurons, but instead of choosing something out of the ordinary for you, you selected a book on a familiar subject, that would not be a unique activity for you. Let's say you like to read about the American Civil War, so you chose another book on the Civil War. You might learn new things, perhaps with some different points of view, but you would be reusing many of the same neural pathways you've used before, each time you had previously read a similar book on the Civil War.

An example of "uniqueness" would be, instead of choosing the third volume of Shelby Foote's trilogy of *The Civil War: A Narrative*, you select something else that would be entirely unique or different, that would inspire and inform a new interest, like *Super Consciousness* by Colin Wilson, or *Kristen Suzanne's Easy Raw Vegan Desserts*.

The rule is: Look for things that are not just new, but are completely unique and out of the ordinary for you.

8. Variety.

In the previous example, I recommended changing your normal habits to create unique new interests. Variety is also important. Avoid sameness. The book reader in the above example might want to read from the Colin Wilson book on Sunday, the book on desserts on Tuesday, and the book on the Civil War on Wednesday.

Or, switch it up even more. You can alternate different activities day to day—from reading, to sculpting, to trail riding, to needlepoint, to planning a trip to Machu Picchu, to volunteering at a shelter. In anything you do, look for diversity, activity, and interests that stimulate or create new neuronal activity in more than one primary area of interest.

9. Emotional content.

Not all neuron builders include strong emotional experience, but the stronger the positive emotions connected with your exercise, the more it will do for you.

Doing something you're passionate about works as an exercise if it isn't something you've done repeatedly in the past. Interest and emotional energy go hand in hand, so I recommend learning as much about your target neuron builders as you can. Learning creates interest, interest creates energy, and energy creates more enthusiasm and emotional involvement. Find things you learn to *love*, not just learn to *like*.

If you've decided that one of your neuron builder exercises is practicing Tai Chi, learn everything about it that you can. Discover where it came from; find out how many forms of Tai Chi there are, and how they differ from each other; research the health benefits you can derive from practicing, and so on. Doing those kinds of things increases the strength of your neuron builder.

If you're exercising your brain by painting in oils, focus on paintings that let you put your heart into them. Paint things you care about. Paint with a purpose. The more you feel, the more of your emotions you're calling on, the more your brain and your mind will grow. And the same holds true, regardless which neuron builders you decide to try. The greater the positive emotions and energy you enjoy during the pursuit, the better it will work.

10. Something you look forward to doing.

Some people who start a new neuron-building program say that the activity is something they always wanted to do. But even if your activity is something new to you, the neuron builders you choose should be so appealing to you that you look forward to the exercises.

These 10 rules will help you build and maintain the habit of using neuron builders in your own everyday life. I encourage you to actively seek out and implement new neuron builders, and apply these rules to each of them. When you do, the rewards you reap will be limited only by your imagination, and the amount of time and energy you invest in each new activity.

Chapter 24

Living "Aware"

When you're exploring the idea of how focused awareness helps the brain grow new neurons, you could divide the world into two groups of people: those who think, and consider, and figure things out—and those who give up, stop thinking, and seldom really exercise their minds at all. There are *aware* people and there are *unaware* people (and those who live somewhere in between).

This isn't about how smart someone is, or even about the amount of education someone has; some of the *least* "aware" people are well educated. It's beyond that. It's about learning to be alive and actively *aware* and *curious*, every day you're here.

Unaware people are not any less important individuals; they've just been programmed to think in a less curious way than more *aware* people think. They're as smart and as capable; they're just living their lives as they learned to live them, in an uninterested way. But I've often thought about the fact that they seem to be missing out on so much. It's as though no one taught the unaware people the one lesson on *paying attention to life* that might have added so much to their lives.

What we see as the *aware* thinkers are the same people who are often healthier, who remain sharper and more in tune with life throughout their entire lives, even into old age.

I'll give you an example of an *unaware* person and an *aware* person.

The person we'll call *"Unaware"* gets up, goes to work, works hard, gets tired, comes home, has dinner, sits down and watches TV, gets more tired, and falls asleep—still "watching" something on television that he won't remember in the morning.

The next day *Unaware* gets up, goes to work, gets tired, goes home and repeats the same old routine again. He will have his "moments," times when he is actually awake and aware of his life and the life that is happening around him— the special birthday, the daughter's wedding, winning the sales contest at work—but for the most part, his brain is running on tired programs. Every day he does nothing truly different or new, so nothing in his brain is being wired to be different or new.

If he keeps it up, he will become a statistic. His mind will die before he does. His heart will fail for lack of interest. And along with the sorrow of losing him, he will, in time, be remembered for nothing more than the fact that he was here for a short while, and then passed on.

The other person, the one we'll call *"Aware,"* gets up in the morning, begins his day with a prayer or meditation, and asks himself the question, "What will I do today to make life better?" (Or he already planned his day the night before.)

He goes to his work, something he enjoys, and he knows his work is the vehicle he has chosen to reach the goals he has set. He may work hard, but his work is not his only focus—his *life* is his focus.

When he goes home after work, he chooses from the myriad of activities that compete for his attention—doing stimulating, fun things with his family, going to his night school class, working on the story line for the novel he has set a goal to write, studying what he will need to know about the hydroponic garden he has started in the greenhouse he built in the back yard, or contacting a friend who needs an uplifting phone call.

With the person who remains *unaware*, the brain "dies." Very slowly, over a lifetime, but that's what it does. The term "use it or lose it" applies all too accurately in this case.

As mentioned earlier, when the brain no longer uses a circuit or pathway, it deletes it, in a process called "pruning." In actual neurological fact, it stops growing or changing, and begins to atrophy.

The unaware brain stops being truly *alive*. It stops being smart, and interested, and hopeful, and mindful of the exceptional opportunities that were awaiting its interest.

With the *aware* person, the brain continues to grow and change—in this case, in a very positive way. The brain of the aware person is *stimulated* to *grow*. And because of his or her interests and activity, that's what it does—day after day, year after year.

We don't know from this short look at their lives, which one of them will live the longest—but we do know which one will live the *most*. *"Aware"* will live a better life than *"Unaware."* Why? Because the human brain does best when it is constantly stimulated, pushed, moved *forward*, forced to tackle new obstacles in new ways, and is continually confronted with new ideas, new opportunities, and new possibilities. Do that for a month, and take note of the results. Do it for a year. Do that for the rest of your life.

The Neuroplastically *Active* Brain

To paraphrase, a brain in motion tends to stay in motion, while a brain at rest tends to stay at rest. That's why active people tend to stay active, and inactive people stay on the couch. It is habit, of course, but it's also the brain doing what you're *wiring* it to do.

When you're mentally active, your brain is more "awake" and aware, and keeps itself sensitized to what's going on in the world around it. When you stay aware, you are identifying many more "moments of attention" than when your brain is indifferent to what's going on around you.

As an example, imagine two people, riding as passengers in two different cars being driven on the exact same route through town. The two cars are driving together, one in front of the other.

In the first car, the *aware* passenger notices many things: how long it's taking the average traffic light to change at each of the intersections the car goes though; which retail stores are open and which are closed; which stores are advertising sales; in a residential area, which lawns are neatly mowed and which are not; whether the school the car passes is open or closed, and on what date the school closed for summer vacation. This passenger notices the name of the song playing

237

on the radio, and who's singing the song; whether the streets are in good repair or need improvement; which billboards are interesting and effective and which ones miss the mark; how many kids are playing on the sidewalks; what the sky is like today, and what that suggests for the weather later on; how many red cars there have been on the road today—and are there more or fewer red cars than usual?

Meanwhile, the *unaware* passenger, riding in the second car and taking the exact same route through town right behind the first car, has a very different drive, and notices almost nothing. This passenger notices only that the red lights seem to be taking too long—and why can't the drive go faster? And that's pretty much it.

Same exact route. Same amount of time. Same opportunities to be alive. Same opportunities to engage the brain. One of the passengers sees *dozens* of things; the other passenger sees almost nothing.

Which of these two passengers' brains has the better chance of staying "alive" longer? It's the first passenger, of course. The second passenger's brain is already shutting down. It has probably been shutting down for a long time.

I'm not suggesting you have to be aware of *everything*— though that's a great neuron-building exercise. But if all other things were equal, the passenger in the first car has a hands-down chance of living a better, more fulfilling life. The first passenger's brain will continue to grow. The other passenger's brain will continue to die.

You can probably think of people you know who are something like the first passenger, and some who are more like the second passenger. But what's most important is, which kind of passenger do *you* choose to be?

You don't always have to be "on." But when you're the one riding somewhere in a car, or walking somewhere, or at work, or just being at home, or thinking about what you'll do tomorrow—how awake, how aware, how interested, how *vital* have you trained your mind to be?

Because we are creatures of habit (or rather, creatures of our programs), we become accustomed to believing that the way we've been living our lives must be a *normal*, acceptable way to keep on living. But what if we're wrong about that?

What if some of the things we're doing are the exact opposite of the things that would make our lives better? What if what we've been doing isn't really creating a better future?

If you'd like your brain to do more things *for* you, consider those things you may be doing now that could be wiring it *against* you. If you'd like to stimulate, excite and grow your brain, here are some things to avoid:

Doing the same thing each day, day in and day out, doesn't work.

Being bored, doesn't work.

Never reading a book, doesn't work.

Never reading a book outside of your personal interests, doesn't work.

Spending useless time online, doesn't work.

Doing the same things this year you did last year, doesn't work.

Always talking about the same things, doesn't work.

239

Refusing to try something new, doesn't work.

Watching endless television, doesn't work.

Never enrolling in a new class or never learning anything new, doesn't work.

Refusing to change, doesn't work.

Having a "Who cares?" attitude, doesn't work.

Believing that "This is just the way I am," doesn't work.

Not setting new goals, doesn't work.

Getting up in the morning and doing nothing new, doesn't work.

Being negative, doesn't work.

Self-medicating to dull stress or anxiety, doesn't work.

Doing nothing of value, doesn't work.

Giving up, doesn't work.

When people feel they have nothing "interesting" to talk about, it's usually because they're not *doing* anything interesting, learning anything new, or thinking interesting *thoughts.*

In a world that is literally filled with interesting things of every description, everywhere around us, some people have trouble coming up with even two or three things that are "interesting." They're not creating any new neural pathways in their brains that give their mind and their future any new paths to follow.

What did the sky look like the last time you saw it? What time is sunrise tomorrow morning? What outfit did your spouse or mate have on when she or he left for work today? What new subject or idea will your mind seize upon today? What will you do or learn that is new or different or "interesting" today?

We have learned that improving the plasticity of our brains is up to us, and each day we're given a thousand chances to practice it and get it right. Here is the kind of thinking that *works:*

Finding interesting, exciting, new things to do, works.

Being open to new ideas, works.

Having faith in your future, works.

Always being keenly observant of the details of the world around you, works.

Staying positive, regardless of the circumstances, works.

Remembering how you felt when you first dreamed about your future, works.

Learning an entirely new skill, works.

Finding and making new friends with new ideas, works.

Studying the room you're in, works.

Setting clear, specific, active new goals and working on them every day, works.

Replacing television with something that demands your thinking, works.

Listening intently and intelligently, instead of talking vacuously, works.

Making a change to a different career, works.

Spending time with inspired people, works.

Believing that you are just beginning, instead of ending, or being stuck where you are, works.

Being inquisitive and asking questions, works.

Reading biographies of inspiring life-changers, works.

Spending time visiting places you've never been, works.

Joining clubs or groups outside of your own interest areas, works.

Looking forward with positive enthusiasm to every tomorrow, works.

Being *Aware* Rewires Your Brain

Can you get up in the morning, get ready, and leave for work without really remembering anything about the hour you spent getting ready? Have you ever shampooed twice, not remembering that you'd already shampooed just a minute ago? Have you ever driven to work without remembering driving to work?

That can happen to any of us. It happens when we allow our brain to go into mental stasis, a state of inactivity during which there is little or no new neuronal activity in the brain, nothing more than maintaining our life-support systems.

A brain in mental stasis is a brain that stays alive, but does not grow. The brain is *"here,"* but isn't participating in *being* here. A brain in mental growth continues to grow and change

If high levels of healthy mental activity are good, then obviously, as the boss of your brain, you can choose activities that will keep your brain in the "mental activity" mode, rather than the "mental stasis" mode.

The kinds of exercises we're discussing in this book can help immensely. Actively practicing them can help you be even more alive, set new goals and be endlessly interested in your tomorrows.

And when you're actively rewiring your brain to see itself as interested, alive, alert, and aware, stimulating your brain will keep it that way!

Being "aware" rewires your brain—for the good.

243

Chapter 25

Making Mindfulness a Way of Life
A 31-Day Way to Change Your Brain

In this chapter, I'm going to give you an exercise I think you'll like, and it will definitely help you wire in a lifelong habit of being mindful.

If you'd like to take advantage of your brain's special neuroplastic power, there is one thing you must do. You have to make your control over your brain's programming process so natural that, for you, being in control and getting positive results will become a way of life.

Although virtually everything we've focused on in this book has been for the purpose of putting you in control of the wiring of your brain, *practicing daily mindfulness of your brain's neuroplasticity* will cement your newly imprinted programs in place. Those new programs will become a part of you, and many of them will become a permanent part of the new neural structure of your brain. That is our intention.

In an earlier chapter, we discussed *mindfulness* as one of the seven key rules for actively rewiring the brain. Here, I'm going to give you some help in making that mindfulness a way of life.

Making mindfulness—the form of metacognition we're talking about here—an automatic part of who you are, could have a profoundly positive effect on your future. This step is designed to help you create the habit of actively *staying mindful* of your role as the absolute manager of your own thoughts—*of you being in charge of your programs.*

The method I recommend to help you stay mindful every day, starts by using daily reminders. This first important step to mindfulness is designed to literally begin to rewire your brain with a new set of *mindfulness programs.*

31 Days of Mindfulness

To take this step, you may want to write the following *"31 Daily Mindfulness Questions"* on 3X5 index cards. If you choose to write them down, carry a new question card with you each day. Read the card three or four times during the day. Read that card once more at the end of the day. Then move that day's question card to the bottom of the deck. The next day, do the same thing with the top card, and repeat the process for all the cards.

You could instead choose to print out the full list of 31 questions, keep the list with you, and read each day's question from the list. That will work as well.

Whichever method you choose, read and answer just *one question* several times each day. The next day, go on to the next question.

As you read through the 31 questions for the first time, here in the book, you'll notice your brain beginning to respond. Listen carefully to the answers you start to get, and the thoughts and ideas that begin to come to your mind. Then imagine the kind of neural pathways you'll be building when you focus on the questions one at a time for the next 31 days—and beyond.

As you focus on the questions each day, you'll also notice your mindfulness is increasing throughout the day. That will be due not only to your focusing on that day's question, but also because you'll be wiring in a new set of neural pathways on mindfulness. And every day those pathways will become stronger.

It would be almost impossible to overstate the importance of teaching yourself mindfulness, and how much it can do for you.

While you're asking the questions and answering them, you'll be more mindful at the moment. But in a short time, by just asking and answering the questions several times each day, you'll be building neural networks that can stay with you for the rest of your life.

It takes time for mindfulness to become a wired-in habit. Set a goal to get started and stay with it. That would be a good 30-day, 60-day, 90-day goal. One month to get started, a second month to build the habit as a natural part of your day, and the third month to make sure it's wired in. Do this one exercise (*ask yourself the questions and answer them*), and stay with it for a minimum of 90 days, and mindfulness will become a lifelong habit.

The 31 Daily Mindfulness Questions:

(**Note**: I've included "Sample Answers" to suggest ideas for the answers *you* choose. You can use these, or put your answers in your own words.)

Day 1. *What can I do today to make myself aware of my own programming?*
(I can ask myself this question *every time I check to see what time it is*—and I can answer the question by saying, "Today I choose to be mindful of my own programming.")

Day 2. *What is the attitude I choose to have all day today?*
(I choose to have a great attitude all day today, and every day.) Or (Today I choose to have a positive attitude about _____.)

Day 3. *What is the #1 program I choose to focus on creating in my brain today?*
(Today I have decided to focus on creating the program to reach my goal of _____.)

Day 4. *How do I know my thoughts and my programs are up to me, and are mine to choose?*
(I know my thoughts and my programs are mine to choose because I'm creating them right now. I'm choosing to give my brain the messages I want to give it.)

Day 5. *How mindful am I of my emotions today?*
(I am aware of programming my brain with positive, healthy emotions. I'm doing that right now.)

Day 6. *What is one thing I can do today to create more positive programs in my brain?*
(I can make sure my *self-talk* is always positive.)

Day 7. *How much do I like myself, love myself, and care about myself today?*
(I have decided to like myself, love myself, and care about myself *incredibly,* today and every day.)

Day 8. *How often am I aware of other people's programs—especially other people's self-talk?*
(I am always aware of other people's programs—especially their self-talk.)

Day 9. *How important do I feel my programs are to my success in anything I do?*
(I know my own programs are one of the most important parts of my success in anything I do.)

Day 10. *How much "in control" of my own programming do I feel today?*
(I am 100% in control of my own programming—today and every day.)

Day 11. *Who is the #1 person who is in control of my mindfulness, my thoughts, my attitude, and my programming today?*
(The #1 person in control of my mindfulness, my thoughts, my attitude, and my programming today—and every day—is *me!*)

Day 12. *What creates my beliefs, my opinions and my direction each day?*
(My beliefs, my opinions and my direction each day are created by my programs—and I'm in charge of my brain and my programs.)

Day 13. *How is my self-talk today?*
(My self-talk today and every day is *on top, in tune, in touch, and going for it!*)

Day 14. *What is the key to making my most positive programs strong and permanent?*
(The key to creating good programs is repetition.)

Day 15. *How can I be mindful today that I have unlimited promise and potential?*
(I just have to tell myself the truth—*I have unlimited promise and potential.* That's me, and that's who I was born to be.)

Day 16. *How important is it for me to be mindful of my thoughts and programs today?*
(My thoughts and my programs are the direction I give to my life. They are *very* important to me, and I choose to be mindful of them—today and every day.)

Day 17. *If I think a negative thought, what is the first thing I do?*
(If I think a negative thought, I immediately replace it with a better, more positive thought. I choose to get rid of the negative and program the positive.)

249

Day 18. *How do I know I was designed to succeed?*
(I know I was designed to succeed because that's the way I was born, and that's the way I was meant to be—and that's the message I give myself every day.)

Day 19. *What do I like most about being mindful, and able to give my mind positive programs that improve my life?*
(I like *everything* about being mindful, and able to give my mind positive programs that improve my life!)

Day 20. *How often each day do I choose to be completely mindful?*
(I choose to mindful all day, every day.)

Day 21. *What is one goal I could set today that will help me be more mindful of my mind, each and every day?*
(I can set a goal to ask myself just before I go to sleep each night, what I did to improve my mind during that day.)

Day 22. *How do I feel about improving my mind and being more aware of all of my thoughts and programs?*
(I'm proud of myself for the amount of time and focus I'm putting into becoming more of the person I want to be.)

Day 23. *What is one thing I can do right now, and throughout the day, to make my mind sharper and more aware?*
(I can notice everything, pay attention to everything, and look for things around me that I've never noticed before. Today I'm focusing on _____.)

Day 24. *What is something I could do for someone else today that would create more positive imprinting in my own programs?*

(I can give an honest compliment to anyone I meet today who looks like they could use a boost.)

Day 25. *How often each day do I program my mind with the positive—by smiling?*
(I program my mind every day with the positive by smiling a *lot*. I smile often, at any time and at every opportunity.)

Day 26. *Who is in control of every thought I think?*
(I am in control of every thought I think.)

Day 27. *Who is in control of my feelings—positive or negative?*
(I am in control of my feelings—positive or negative. And I choose *positive!*)

Day 28. *What is the first thing I think about each morning, and the last thing I think about each night?*
(I always focus my thoughts on something good, peaceful, thankful, and positive.)

Day 29. *What is one of the greatest gifts I have ever received for making my life better?*
(One of the greatest gifts I have ever received for making my life better—is the ability to create my future with my mind.)

Day 30. *What is the best way to create the habit of staying mindful?*
(Since creating the habit of being mindful comes from practicing being mindful each day, I have made the choice to use this list of daily reminders often.)

Day 31. *What is the key to making my own mindfulness a way of life for me?*
(The key to making my own mindfulness a way of life for me is practice, practice, practice; with repetition, repetition, repetition. And I look forward to doing that, every day.)

That is a month of daily "mindfulness" questions. If you ask yourself those simple questions several times each day for one month, you'll increase your mindfulness of your role as the person who is responsible for wiring and nurturing your brain. When you go beyond the first month, you'll begin to wire your mindfulness in place in your brain. And if you go on from there, and stay with it as I've suggested, your mindfulness will be assured.

Now is the Right Time to Begin

I've found from working with people over many years that sometimes those who truly want to follow even the simplest of steps (like asking themselves the 31 questions), or following any other regimen for personal growth, can fail to do so. As a result, they miss the opportunities their new steps could have helped them find.

At the moment most of these people learned about their "opportunity steps" (like when they read them in a book), they were not only in agreement, but they were excited about putting them into practice. Three days later they had forgotten them. That's not really their fault, or a lack of interest on their part. It's old programs.

To defeat those old programs now, I encourage you to set an absolutely unstoppable goal to ask yourself the questions I've suggested to you—one question several times each day—beginning today. And choose a reward for yourself when you've done so. No forgetting, and no excuses.

You and your future are worth far more than the small amount of time and dedication it will take you to read, and answer, just one of those questions a few times each day.

If you do that, you will begin to achieve the results you wanted to reach by reading this book in the first place. And you will benefit greatly from the results.

The "31 Daily Mindfulness Questions" from this chapter are available as a printable PDF, so you can download the questions and use them in place of writing out the individual cards. The download address is:

www.shadhelmstetter.com/mindfulness.

Chapter 26

Meditation, Neuroplasticity, and the Brain

Meditation changes the physical structure of your brain.

People who are exceptionally adept at meditation are able to control their minds so completely that they can change their heartbeat, control their blood pressure, change their body temperature, and override the unconscious and complex system of their body's internal organs. And they are able to do all this with their *thoughts*.

Meditation, as we're discussing it here, is not a spiritual practice but a focusing tool for the mind, to help you become healthier, both mentally and physically. And it is an important tool for improving your neuroplastic programming.

(If you choose to use meditation as part of a spiritual practice, it will continue to work for you when it is combined with the concepts we're discussing here. The goal here is to introduce or affirm the practice of meditation as a healthy programming practice that anyone can use.)

Because of rigorous laboratory testing, meditation has become a part of our scientific understanding of how the mind works, and what each of us can do to exercise more control over our minds and bodies. Today, any study of the effects of our thoughts on our neuroplasticity has to seriously consider what science has learned from the study of the practice of meditation.

Even before scientists got interested, a lot of other people had already figured out that meditation deserved serious attention.

Many Tai Chi, Taekwondo, and other martial arts programs include meditation in their training. Meditation is central to the practice of Yoga. Psychologists recommend meditation to their clients. Most wellness trainers consider meditation a must. Life coaches recommend meditation as a way for their clients to quiet the outer mind, and access the positive programs of the inner mind.

As scientific research has begun to prove the benefits that meditation offers to our overall health and well-being, medical doctors are more and more often recommending meditation to their patients. After all the countless years meditation has been practiced and its benefits clearly shown, in our "enlightened" time, meditation has been welcomed into the mainstream of popular culture.

This is because science finally proved that thoughts rewire the brain. And one of the most immediate and direct ways to prove that, was by studying people who meditate, and by studying them *while* they're meditating.

Because of what science is continuing to prove about meditation and its physical and mental effects on the neuron structure of the brain, in a few years from now, there won't

255

be a health and wellness program that does not include some form of meditation. The bottom line is this: *meditation creates positive neuronal growth in your brain.* If you want to think better, live better, have more control, be more alive each day, and get more in touch with the real you, then you will want to create the time to meditate each day.

To Begin: A First-Step Meditation

This is a first-step meditation that will help you get started rewiring your brain in a relaxed, positive way. Even if we had not learned that the practice of meditation was directly connected to the restructuring of your brain, I would have recommended it to you just to help you relax, get focused, and face life each day in a calmer, more intelligent and more mindful way. But as we've found, meditating each day can be much more than that.

If you already practice meditation at a level beyond what I'm suggesting here, keep doing what you're doing. You're likely already changing your neural pathways and adding healthy new programs. What you learn here about neuroplasticity and the mind will enhance your understanding and your meditation. If you're not already practicing meditation in some form that works for you, the "first-step" method I share with you here will get you started.

Many people have found the only hurdle to get past in meditating is just that—getting started. This is simply because we're so busy, we put off taking care of ourselves until we've taken care of everything else we think we have to take care of first. But let's assume you *get it*, that you know you're *worth* it, and you really want to try it.

As you first read the following steps and try them for yourself, you'll notice they're designed to be simple and easy to do.

When asked how many minutes each day a beginning meditator should take to meditate, I would give the same answer physical trainers give to their new, sometimes out-of-shape adults students: If you want to start walking a mile or more each day, start with walking for even a few steps a day. This meditation exercise is about getting started—so to begin with, meditating a few minutes at a time is fine.

1. Find the time and the place.

If you're going to meditate for even a few minutes to begin with, you'll have to find the time and the place to do so. You'll need a quiet room or a place with no distractions or interruptions. For beginners, lights should be low.

You should plan for your startup period to take 3 to 4 weeks. If you want this to work, you should make sure you have a time and space available to you for at least that time. It can take that long for your brain to begin to build permanent new neural pathways that stay with you.

When you meditate properly, you are *not* just quieting your mind for the moment; when you stay with it, you are literally creating new neural programs that will continue to work on your behalf, getting you closer to controlling the chemicals of your mind, long after you are through meditating each day.

2. Sit in a comfortable position.

You don't have to be in a traditional "lotus" position to meditate. Sitting with your palms "up" and open is good, because you're telling your physical self you are receptive to positive input. (However, if you choose not to do that, don't worry about it. This isn't so much about what disciplined meditators might do; this is more about you meditating, and making it work.)

For now, simply sit in a comfortable chair with your legs in a comfortable position, and your spine reasonably straight.

3. Close your eyes, and relax.

When we're going to sleep each night we close our eyes—but we don't always relax. So this is something you may have to create some new neural pathways in order to do well. This step just asks you to do it. The next step will help.

Because your brain is creating new neural pathways dedicated to intentional relaxation, this will become easier each time you practice.

4. Take slow, deep breaths.

Begin by breathing slowly in and out. Count slowly as you breathe in. Count slowly again, as you breathe out. Don't worry about whether you're doing it perfectly. Just breathe in and out, deeply and slowly.

5. Focus your attention.

Doing this might be confusing when you're first getting started. This is why beginners are sometimes guided to focus on an image like a mandala, or on the imagined flame of a single candle glowing in the darkness.

Find a center point in your mind, with your eyes closed. Concentrate on that point in your mind's eye.

Don't worry if this isn't easy at first. Focusing is a skill, something that has to be learned. When you practice, you'll be forming new neural pathways in your brain that will get stronger, and focusing will become easier.

6. Say one word in your mind.

This is optional, but it can help profoundly, especially with the beginning meditator. Not every meditator uses a significant word to help them focus. But for now, know that the word you use will tie your meditation to other, similar neural circuits in your mind, so it can be very helpful to do this.

As an example, your word can be something like *"peace," "harmony," "love," "forgiveness," "acceptance," "compassion," "understanding," "oneness," "wellness," "purpose," "guidance," "faith," "belief," "focus,"* or any other uplifting, positive word you choose.

Just select a word you'd like to focus on at the moment. Your word can change each time you meditate, or you can focus on the same word for as long as you choose.

7. Empty your mind.

(Well, not entirely, but almost.)

As you begin, let everything go, and think of nothing, other than the focus word you've chosen. The idea is to ignore past and future thoughts, and connect to the moment you're in now.

Stay focused on your center point. If you're new to meditating, asking you to think of "nothing" is asking your mind to do something you may never have asked it to do before. For now, if you start to think any one of those outside thoughts—about breakfast, work, the kids, your appointment—let the thought pass. Just let it come in and go out. Don't ask it to stay, but don't fight it, either. Go back to your focus word.

For some people, other than getting started and actually meditating, this could seem like the most difficult part. But as you practice, you'll find your mind clearing more easily.

This quiet clarity and space within is also one of the most rewarding parts of meditating. When was the last time you thought of nothing at all, other than a single thought, or word, or question? Imagine a space in your mind with no clutter, no noise, no anything—not like an idle brain lapse, but actually *nothing* at all—and let your own brain become aware of itself. This is you, getting to listen to you.

8. Listen.

Keep breathing slowly, relax, and *listen*.

It may take some time to get to the silence and then the message. But if you keep doing it, when you listen, you will begin to hear your inner self, or your "higher" self talking to you. Usually, after a time of listening, you'll hear the quiet, or the silence, or the message you were waiting for.

Wait this out, but don't grasp. Let it come naturally. Most of us aren't used to waiting. We've trained ourselves to fill every minute with *something*. So our brains aren't used to waiting, or listening to nothing. Each time you meditate, you'll be training your body to relax and your mind to wait and to listen, and in time, you'll be perfectly at ease doing this.

If you like, you can ask a question in the silence. Many people, while they're meditating, have almost a conversation with their "higher" self. What's interesting about the answers they get is that they are almost always very short, very clear, very simple, and they are often right on target.

9. *Relax completely, and stay with it.*

Breathe again, deeply, counting your breaths in, and counting them out. Stay with your meditation for as long as you can. The more you practice meditating, the longer you'll be able to stay in the relaxed, peaceful place you're creating.

Then, after you've stayed in this place in your mind for a time, when you're ready to return from your meditation, you'll know. If you want to stay longer, stay longer. The inner peace you'll begin to feel is a part of you that has been waiting for you to find it.

10. *Reflect.*

As you're coming out of your meditation, make the choice to keep the peaceful attitude of mind you've been creating. As you do this, ask yourself the clear question,

"What did I learn?" Listen carefully to every answer that comes into your mind.

(Don't worry if nothing comes to you. Meditation is characterized by *letting go* of expectations or requirements. Your practice of it will be unique to *you*.)

Then remain very still, open your eyes, keep breathing slowly and think about everything you just felt, saw, and learned. Be completely mindful. Reflect on your meditation and what it means to you now. Continue to exit your meditation slowly. Readjust to where you are, and stretch. "Like" where you are, think of the gift of life you have, nod your head "yes" to your future, and smile.

At this time, decide when you will next meditate, choose to do it, and agree with yourself that you will meditate at that time. This will increase the anticipation and help you create the habit more quickly.

The Benefits of Meditating Go Far Beyond the Meditation Itself

This simple exercise of meditation I've suggested here is not an esoteric practice in any way. It is a way to quiet the world, and connect to your mind and your brain in a very practical, direct way.

The goal is to increase your ability to tune in to you, listen to your "self" in a clear, uncluttered time, and gain the advantage of a relaxed "peace of mind" you can take with you into the rest of your everyday life. In so doing, you will be rewiring your mind in some very positive ways.

When you meditate, you're going to love the *centering*, the *mindfulness*, the *relaxation*, the *serenity*, the *positive uplift* of your self and the *answers* that will come to you. But the greatest benefits often occur outside of the meditation itself. Here's what to look for:

More mindfulness throughout each day
Increased self-awareness
Increased awareness of your health and habits
A calmer attitude overall
A better understanding of others
More patience
Lower stress
A greater interest in improving yourself
A greater interest in helping others

These and other benefits will come to you. Once you've done it for a while, if you ever stop, you will probably think, *I should do that again. I should meditate. That was very good for me.*

Why can you be so certain? Because while you're practicing, *you'll be wiring the habit of meditation into your brain.* And every step you practice is designed not only to be a good meditation tool, but also a neurological tool designed to help your brain wire in that habit effectively and efficiently.

What will make it work the best? *Repetition, repetition, repetition.*

Happy meditating!

Chapter 27

The Transformational Retreat

So far, in this book, I've told you that you were born with unlimited promise and potential; that you're probably smarter than you realized; that any old programs that have been stopping you can be erased and replaced, and that you can literally program your success in virtually anything that is possible to do or achieve. Because of the power of neuroplasticity, all of that is fact.

And that means that *what you choose next* suddenly becomes very important.

This chapter recommends something you can do to make sure that all of your programming from here on out is on the right track, and takes you where you want to go. It's something many of the most successful people I know, do when they want to reset their sights and make sure they're firmly in control of their own future.

Since your neuroplastic programming future is up to you, if you're going to put yourself in charge of your brain and your mind, it will be important to know exactly where you want to go and what you'd most like to do with every day of the incredible life you have in front of you.

What would you choose to do with the rest of your life if you knew you could do it? Here are some important questions to ask:

What would you like to do with the next 5 years of your life?

The next 3 years?

The next year?

What is the basis of your belief in yourself? Good or bad, where did it come from?

From yourself?

Did someone else tell you how good you were or what you could do?

Are there any old doubts you have about yourself that came from old programs? And do any of those programs still hold you back or stop you?

Is there anything about yourself or your life that you'd like to change, if you could?

Are you living each day the way you'd like to be, in your relationships?

Are you living each day the way you'd like to be physically, and with your health?

Are you living each day the way you'd like to be spiritually?

If there is something you'd really like to do but you haven't yet done, do you know what's stopping you?

If there is, do you know what to do about that?

Do you know what your skills and talents really are?

Have you used all your skills and perfected most of them?

Is there a talent you think you might have, that you've never done anything with?

Are you doing, every day, what makes you happiest?

Is there something else you'd rather be doing with your life?

When you arrive at the end of your days, will you have done what you really came here to do?

If there is one thing you'd like to do next, what is it?

Do you know exactly where you really want to go, and how to get there?

If you could wave your wand, and do absolutely anything that is possible, what would it be?

The fact is, most of the people we will ever meet will get up tomorrow, get ready for the day, and go through it without a single thought about *who they really are* and *what they would really like to be doing* with the rest of their lives. And they'll get up the following day and do the same.

All too many people go through their entire lifetimes doing that. People who live a life which is not driven by purpose, with nowhere in particular to go, see no reason to take the time to plan their own futures or to make clear choices to help them find and fulfill their destinies.

Others, however, understand that life, for them, should not be left up to chance or serendipity. They want to know what their purpose is, and how to live it and move forward in the best possible way.

With our new knowledge that our brains will *help us grow and change* (and that the brain is designed to do that), we suddenly have a whole new way to look at what we can do next.

Taking the Time to Find out Who You Are, and Where You're Going

When was the last time you spent a weekend, or even an entire day, having someone focus *entirely* on *you* and what you want to do with the rest of your life?

I'm not talking about just getting ahead or doing a little better in one area or another of your life. The kind of personal experience I will share with you here is about your *destiny.* It's about something you can do to help you find that destiny, and then chart a course that actually takes you there.

267

One of the very best ways I've ever discovered to find out where you are now, and the path you'd like to take next, is called the *"transformational retreat."*

Over a number of years, as I've shared this process with people, I've watched their lives change as a result. My own path in life, on more than one occasion, has been given vibrant new life—simply because I invested the time to go through the steps it took to review and reset my course. The transformational retreat has always proved to be a very powerful and effective way to chart a life course.

I still personally conduct transformational retreats (which are modestly called "The Shad Helmstetter Transformational Retreat"), and I have also trained a select few individuals how to correctly moderate those retreats.   In the next few pages, I will show you how to experience a personalized version of the retreat for yourself, by giving you an insight into the tools and techniques that will help you do that. Holding a transformational retreat is something I really love to do; it can be incredibly life-changing—and when you try it for yourself, I believe you're going to love it too.

The reason the transformational retreat can be so life-changing is that it sets up the perfect environment for identifying the direction you would most like the neuroplasticity of your brain to follow—the direction you'd like your life to take. It asks you exactly the right questions, and helps you find your future path within the answers you give.

To give you an example of this, in the transformational retreats I conduct, at the beginning of the first day, the first question I ask is: *"What name were you given on the day you were born?"*

268

That's where it begins. From that first moment on, throughout a full day and evening, I continue to ask the right questions to take the participants through every meaningful point in their lives, and bring them to the present moment.

Then, after the participants answer each of the questions in their own words, when they have a complete picture of their lives so far—including what worked and what didn't—I ask them the final question of the night: *"If you could do anything you wanted to do with the rest of your life, starting now, if you could do anything that is possible—wave your wand, and answer the question—what would it be?"*

The participants don't get to answer the question that night; they have to wait until morning to answer it. With that question burning in their minds, they often don't get a lot of sleep that night.

That's because, after seeing a completely objective review of their lives so far, they are now coming into direct contact with their own *futures*, and the immense and amazing possibilities that are in front of them now. They're about to find the answers. And it's those answers that change their lives, often in wondrous ways.

Earlier, we discussed the importance of creating the *focus* necessary to wire in clear programming networks in the brain. The transformational retreat takes that focus to a whole new level.

In the chapter on *choices*, we learned that many people spend more time choosing the clothes they wear than they spend choosing the life they truly want to live. The problem has been that most people don't know how to find out what they really want. They're too busy getting by and getting older to figure out what they could really be doing with the life they

269

have in front of them. That's exactly what the transformational retreat is for.

The Way it Works Best

Here is an overview that will help you plan a personal retreat. In its most effective form, the transformational retreat looks like this:

1. Begin by making the decision to take 1 to 3 days for the retreat. One full day and night, at a minimum; 2 days is better. The third day is recommended but optional. It is for reflection and creative brainstorming.

2. *Very important:* Hold your retreat in a location that is away from your home, and where the noise and mental clutter of any busy environment are absent. It should be held at a location that will feel completely peaceful, uplifting and positive.

When I personally conduct a retreat, I select a location for my participants that is wide open and airy, with a lot of windows, such as a condo overlooking a beach or somewhere with visually distant horizons. (One of my favorite parts of my time with the attendees is when we are able to walk together on the same kind of quiet beach I chose when I was writing my first book. It's an amazing part of the process to witness and share what happens when their horizons begin to open up—in some cases, for the first time ever.)

Your retreat location can be anywhere, but wherever you choose, it should feel "right." While you're there, you're going to be finding paths, opening up your future, and creating directions that could well change the rest of your life; make sure the place you choose lends itself to limitless inspiration.

3. Write and bring with you a list of the most important questions you can think of, whose answers will help you paint the picture of your perfect future. (If you'd like to know the best way to word your questions, you can refer to the download link of sample questions I've included at the end of this chapter.)

4. The main tools you'll need to take with you are a stand-up easel, a large pad of paper (I recommend a fresh 27 x 34-inch graph paper pad) that you'll place on the easel, and a handful of colored felt-tipped pens. You'll be using different colors for different things that are written on the easel pad. Also, bring favorite snacks and beverages. This is going to be a very exciting but very relaxed weekend, so plan on being comfortable.

5. Another tool I recommend you bring with you is a music player and selections of your favorite relaxing or emotionally uplifting music. Music is not essential for everyone, but the right music helps lift people out of the ordinary and into the realm of unlimited possibilities, so I always have the right music playing in the background.

6. Select, carefully, the *one* person you'll ask to attend your retreat with you. This will be the facilitator or moderator. The

person who joins you *must* be someone you trust implicitly. That can be a spouse, or mate, or a trusted friend.

Your retreat partner must agree to follow the retreat rules—such as, he or she is not allowed to give *any* criticism—not even a raised eyebrow—of any ideas you express during the retreat. Another rule is: *no opinions are allowed* from the facilitator unless you specifically ask for them. This is not about someone *else's* agenda for *your* life.

During the retreat, the facilitator will be asking you carefully sequenced, pre-written questions. When you answer each question, your facilitator will write your answers on the easel pad in front of you—in most cases, word for word. You'll have time to think through each answer you give, so when your facilitator writes your answer on the pad, you will get an accurate picture of your responses.

Other than being 100% positive at all times, your facilitator will do two things during the focus hours of your retreat: *a)* Ask you questions from a pre-written list, and *b)* Write each of your final answers on the easel pad. During off periods during the retreat, the facilitator will also be there for whatever discussions the question-and-answer process inspires.

(It will be essential that your facilitator not give you advice unless you ask for it. With a highly outgoing, expressive partner, you may have to have him or her sign an *oath* to keep *their* opinions to themselves.)

What's most important is for your partner to be there as a facilitator, not a counselor. The questions your partner asks are designed to take you through your entire path in life—every key step of where you've been, to where you are now, to where you'd like to go next—in each key area of your life.

The questions will be the guide, and your facilitator should follow them. Your answers will create the observations, the conclusions, the epiphanies (the "Aha!"s) and the direction you're seeking.

Imagine sitting comfortably, completely relaxed but at the same time focused, having the time to think carefully about each question your facilitator asks. You're probably gazing out the window at the beautiful, peaceful ocean waves or other uplifting setting you've chosen for your retreat.

Without criticism or comment, your facilitator writes each of your answers in colored pens on the easel pad. You're never rushed, and you take your time. You have time to tune in to your true self, and as you discover and reveal your own answers, one by one, your next steps become clear.

It's an exciting, positive, revealing time that is all about you. And you will never forget it.

At the end of the retreat, the pages from the easel pad, filled in with your answers, are given to you. When you hold these pages, you are literally holding much of your life and, very possibly, an important part of your future in your hands.

Sharing the Retreat Time

In setting up your retreat, you may want to share the retreat 50/50 with your partner. That is, on a 3-day retreat, as an example, for a full day and a half, the retreat is focused entirely on you, and is all about you and only you. For the other day and a half of the retreat, you change roles, and you become the facilitator, asking the questions and writing out the answers your partner gives. Now the retreat becomes completely about the other person.

Either way, whether sharing the retreat or having the entire time focus entirely on you, when you plan your retreat, you should prepare in advance to leave behind any concerns you have about taking time just for you. Your part of the retreat will focus on you, and it's essential that it remains entirely on you throughout your part of the retreat time.

That is not for a moment being selfish or self-centered in any negative way. It is that focus *on you* that is essential to making the retreat work. (You deserve the time. After all, you've spent a lot of years focusing on everything and everyone else; now it's time for *you*.)

The result of your retreat, no matter what revelations and directions you end up with, will be—perhaps for the first time in your life—a complete list of "life instructions" that you will be handing to the powerful neuroplastic planning department of your brain.

As we've now seen, your brain is designed to act on the specific directions you give it. Because of neuroplasticity, your brain will act just as readily and powerfully on the *right* directions as it does on the *wrong* directions. *Your retreat will help you make sure you're giving your brain the right directions.*

The Importance of Taking Time to Focus on You

The retreat can not only help you find the clearest path to your own goals, but will also help you actualize the dreams and aspirations you have that will help everyone around you that you care about most. The positive results of your transformational retreat will do as much for them as it will do for you.

In my work in the field of personal growth, I've had the opportunity to personally conduct retreats many times as the retreat facilitator—the one who asks the questions. As a result, I've seen the people who went through the retreat process go on to do amazing things in their lives. And each of them say it was that one personal retreat, focused entirely on them, that gave them their real direction and changed their future.

Earlier in this chapter, I asked the question: *"When was the last time you spent a weekend, or even a day, having someone focus entirely on you, and what you want to do with the rest of your life?"*

If you haven't done that, it's time you did!

I've never met any goal-oriented individual, who learns about the process of discovery that the transformational retreat offers them, that doesn't want to experience it for themselves. I hope you'll plan a retreat weekend for yourself, as soon as you can schedule it.

To download a sample list for your personal use, of the kinds of questions I use when I conduct a transformational retreat, or to receive a schedule of retreats you can attend, go to www.shadhelmstetter.com/transformationalretreat.

Chapter 28

Super-Charging the Next 6 Weeks

I have created a special support tool for you to immediately begin implementing the ideas we're discussing in this book. It's something that's easy to do, it doesn't cost you anything, it's extremely helpful, and anyone can do it. It will definitely get you started and super-charge your next few weeks.

This support tool will help you start putting the ideas presented in this book into practice. It will also help you stay with it, keep moving forward, stay focused, and track your progress.

The tool is a six-week in-home coaching program that you'll receive by email, called *"The Neuroplasticity Coach —Six Weeks to Success."* It's designed for you to use as an adjunct to this book.

As soon as you begin using this tool, it will help you *wire in* the right goals and give you additional support in reaching them. (It is the important first few weeks of *practicing* positive neuroplasticity that puts the ideas into motion, gives them life, creates the habit of following through, and begins to make them work.)

Because the coaching modules consist of six weekly home coaching sessions, the program itself is too lengthy to fit into this book. Instead, I've made the program available as a direct download. (As a reader of this book, you'll receive all six weekly coaching sessions at no cost.)

In each week's home coaching session, I'll be asking you exactly the right coaching questions. I'll also be giving you additional ideas, suggestions and support to help you reach each of the goals you set.

The weekly coaching modules will help you create the habit of *mindfulness*, while they help you make *choices*, define your *intention*, fine tune your *focus*, practice self-talk through *repetition*, and give life to your goals with positive *emotion* and *belief*—the seven rules we've discussed in this book for wiring positive programs into place.

Each week you'll be coached to stay on target, keep your focus, set your goals and take action steps. And most important, you'll have the opportunity to *train your brain* and create new neural pathways of the positive kind.

To receive a download of the coaching program *"Six Weeks to Success,"* go to www.shadhelmstetter.com/sixweekstosuccess.

Chapter 29

What Tomorrow May Bring

In summary of this amazing discovery of the power of neuroplasticity in our own personal growth, there are a few points I encourage you to keep with you.

The discoveries go beyond what we've talked about here, of course. Ongoing research in the brain's neuroplasticity is opening exciting new vistas in health, medicine, education, physical therapy, counseling, and beyond. We still have much to learn, because it is a field that, in many ways, is only just beginning.

But we have already learned a lot. It is literally life-changing to apply the discovery of neuroplasticity in one incredibly important area of your life—the area of taking personal *control* of your personal *growth*.

This one discovery gives you the scientific understanding to have a great deal more personal control over your own mind, your brain, and your future. You may not be able to predict the future, but using what we've learned, you can make a profound difference in what that future holds for you.

Imagine what you could do with a brain that: *is always clear, sharp, and alert; thinks in the positive; deals with problems, but refuses to be stopped by them; believes in your unlimited potential and inspires you to reach it; is endlessly encouraging; will do for you what you tell it to do, and is neurologically hard-wired to succeed.*

If you choose it, that is the brain you can have. That is a picture of the amazing future you have in front of you as a result of the power of neuroplasticity, and the discovery that the restructuring of your brain's neural pathways is up to you.

This is the goal that every researcher in the field of personal growth for more than half a century has worked to achieve—to give the control of *you,* and your personal potential, back to *you.*

With new discoveries in the field of neuroplasticity continuing to unfold, we don't yet know how far our new awareness will take us. As of now, we know this:

1. You are in charge.

It's not your genes; it's not what you may have believed about yourself in the past; it's not your parents or your family; it's not your friends; it's not the biases or the level of your education, it's not your job or career path, and it's not what you see on television or what happens randomly in your everyday life, that is in charge of you.

If you choose to take control, *you* will be in charge. You and your programming will be the direct result of your thoughts, your self-talk, what you desire most, and what you choose to do next.

2. The "input" you give your brain will form the neural pathways that you choose.

What an amazing, life-altering discovery this is! You create the right input—new thoughts, new ideas, new awareness, new actions—and your brain will record that input and create it as reality in your mind.

Napoleon Hill's famous adage, *"Whatever the mind can conceive and believe, it can achieve,"* has been brought to life with our new understanding of the role of every thought you think, every goal you set, and every attitude you choose. You were born and created to live an exceptional life, and it has become neurologically clear that living that life is up to you and your programs—not up to luck, coincidence, or the limited beliefs of others.

3. With the help of neuroplasticity, you get to create positive changes in your mind, your brain and your life.

You get to change or improve, both *internally* and *externally*, more of what happens next, by your choice. You get to direct your goals, your attitudes, and your beliefs— and with that, your actions, your results, and your future. You get to change your mind and your brain. And you get to do all that with science solidly on your side.

4. Through repetition, your brain will create strong new neural pathways, and delete harmful old pathways.

This is perhaps the most exciting news of all. Not only will your brain create new programs, it will also *delete* old programs that work *against* you.

When you want to tone up your body, you do physical exercises. You do those exercises repeatedly until you reach the level of muscle strength and tone you want to achieve. That's because we know the key to any good physical regimen, and what makes it work, is *repetition*.

The same is true of the programming process in the brain—especially when it comes to improving what you can do in any important area of your life. Just like improving yourself physically, in personal growth, the more you repeat the same thought or action, the stronger that neural program pathway will be wired into your brain.

When you do that, your brain begins to override old pathways that programmed you to do something in the "old" way. In time, the old paths are *deleted* as you create new roads to follow—*new neural pathways*. When each new pathway is strong enough, through repetition, it becomes the pathway your brain will follow. And that becomes the new *you*.

5. Your goals and your intentions take on an important new meaning.

It's unfortunate that goal-setting is not taught early, both at home and in the first grades of every school. Our clearly-defined goals send signals to the brain that say, "*This* is the path I want to follow." *Your brain records your intention. Your brain records your goals.* And with your focus and your action, your brain helps you achieve the goal.

It has often been said that the brain is a goal-seeking mechanism. It will always try to do what you want it to do. Your *goals* and your *intention,* clearly defined, become some of the most primary and important directions to your brain that it will ever receive.

We now know that not only does your brain *listen,* it also takes *action* on whatever you tell it most often and most clearly.

6. Your attitude is a choice. The attitude you choose each day will determine the quality and success of every day you live.

One great attitude, on one average day, won't change your life. But a year of those incredible, brain-changing, life-enhancing attitudes *will.* And it takes only a matter of days to get that year established on the right track.

We have learned that not only is your attitude a "choice" that you can make each day, but it is also a neurological habit: neural pathways, imprinted with states of mind you can call upon at any time. Your attitude controls many of the chemical switches that tell you how you feel, how you're doing physically, and what and how you think at any given moment.

Your attitude literally controls the outcome of your day, each and every day. And you can control and change that outcome with the single decision to create the attitude of your choice.

7. Your success in actively rewiring neural programs in your brain will depend on seven scientifically important rules.

The brain rewires itself best when you follow the seven guidelines that have been defined by scientific research. They are, as I have identified them in this book, *Mindfulness, Choices, Intention, Focus, Repetition, Emotion,* and *Belief.*

If you practice those seven vital programming elements, you'll change the wiring of your brain, and thereby change the attitudes, beliefs, and actions that will determine the outcome of your life.

8. Your self-talk will be a critically important factor in determining your success in your future.

At one time, many people thought that "self-talk" was nothing more than the idle and unimportant ramblings of thoughts that come and go in your mind. Self-talk, as we now know, with the latest science behind it, is much more important than that; in fact, your self-talk is *extremely* important.

You can't think a *negative thought* without recording it in your brain. You can't think a *positive thought* without recording it in your brain. This one requirement to doing better every day, and creating a better future in everything you do, has become an indisputable scientific fact.

If you're not devotedly practicing positive self-talk in your life every day, I encourage you to do so. Your self-talk should become so rich, so clear, so detailed, so strong, and so positive that *nothing*, at any time or in any way, can hold you back or stop you from becoming the incredible individual you were destined to be.

If you have a goal to improve something in your life, it will be your self-talk that takes you there. Beyond everything else, we now know that your *self-talk* literally creates and wires your programs, and it profoundly influences and controls your thoughts, your ideas, your beliefs, your feelings, your attitudes, and your actions.

The self-talk you learn through repetition, and record in your brain, virtually directs and shapes your days and your future from the opportunities that make up your life.

The Force of Your "Will"

No matter how deeply neuroscientists have searched, they haven't yet been able to find your personal "will," in any easily-identifiable location in your brain.

Your "will" is not in the amygdala, the part of the brain that causes you to be alerted to danger, and deal with the syndrome of "fight or flight." Your "will" is not located in the hippocampus, which helps you create and store memories. It's not in the hypothalamus, which deals with your autonomic nervous system and affects the activity of the pituitary gland. Your "will" is not found anywhere in the cerebral cortex or in any single area of the brain that we know of.

Yet, somehow, your "will," the force that drives you, is found in, and rises above, all of these normal, important, productive parts of the brain that we live with.

Your "will" is your "spirit of life." It is your "will" that urges you onward. It reminds you there is a better way, when you are accepting less than the best of who you could become. It is your "will" that drives you forward, when life, or those around you, would hold you back.

What happens when your dreams, your goals, and your "will" all come together in your life? The answer is, when your greatest dreams, your goals, and your "will" come together, the "magic" happens. That is when life has meaning, when you know for certain you have purpose and value, and that there is a direction in your life you cannot ignore.

Your "will" is that part of yourself which takes you beyond the everyday, and makes you long for the better picture of a life you somehow sense could be in front of you. It is because of your "will," that you can believe in your greatest dreams.

The "will" that you have to rise beyond the ordinary, may not be a part of your brain at all. It may be a part of you that we can only call your "mind" or your "spirit."

Wiring Your Brain for Life

As I have studied and written about the power we have to direct and utilize the vast capabilities of the brain, I have been given the gift of time and experience to see for myself the result of what happens when people make the choice to get it right.

Wire your brain for what you want and what is good, and you very likely will get it and live it out in the rest of your life.

In my own mind and in my own life, I began my journey with a goal to reach people in a way that would count. I wanted to speak and write about things that helped, instead of things that didn't. The path I've followed has been long, and it has had its roadblocks and setbacks. But because I decided to wire my thinking with a belief in the best, and demanded of myself that I not give up or give in, I have continued my quest to accomplish my goal: *reach people, send help.*

During the writing of this book, I have, many times, stood on the deck of a country pavilion that sits next to a small lake on the peaceful Florida wild land where I live. It is surrounded by a beautiful landscape of white three-rail fences, horse pastures, grass-covered meadows, and natural land that is my home.

The centerpiece of the pavilion is a picturesque, wedding-cake gazebo that stands on the deck, over the water. I designed the lakeside pavilion and had it built so my family would have a place to gather, and I would have a place at home to write near the water.

At sunset, the small lake turns to crimson and gold. The fish in the lake, the brim and the wise old uncatchable bass, swim safely beneath the surface. The squirrels play in the trees along the creek that makes its way past the quiet little lake.

When I'm there, in that solitude by the water, especially late in the evening as the stars come out, I usually think of three things.

One is how peaceful it is.

Another is how fortunate I feel, after all these years, to be able to experience turning the dreams of my earlier, shoeless youth into the abundance of my today. If I could overcome the early circumstances of my own life, I know that anyone else can overcome theirs.

And the third thing I think is about what I will write today or tomorrow to share what I've learned with every person who might read what I have to say.

The message I've chosen to tell the world is the message that is the most important to me, for what it can do for others. It is a message that is psychologically sound, steeped in endless scientific research, tested and proved, and filled with incredible hope.

The message is: *You determine your tomorrow, with every thought you think, today.*

The Miracle that is "You"

You were designed, from birth, to succeed.

Let me repeat that: *You were designed, from birth, to succeed.*

You were that infant in that bassinet, perhaps in some newborn nursery, so many years ago, with your eyes wide open, looking for your future, searching for your purpose, and waiting to live out your life of unlimited potential.

You are still that person today. You may be older, more experienced, and either lifted up or pulled down by life's challenges. But you are still that miracle of creation that was born to live a life of value, worth, promise, and unlimited potential.

That will never go away.

Along the way, some of your programs may have held you back. That's what some programs do. But whoever you are now, wherever you are now at this time in your life, you can change almost anything about yourself and your own view of life that you want to change.

287

Keep the best of it. Hold on to the "you" that you like most. Stay with the things that work. But *change* any programs you have that work against you. If there is something you have lived with for a lifetime that no longer works, or if you would like to change in a way that would make your life better—go ahead, *rewire your brain in the way you would like your life to be.*

You are so much more than you can possibly imagine. What an incredible gift you have. What an amazing life you can create! It's all up to you, and every next thought you choose to think.

The next time you have the opportunity, on a crystal-clear starlit night, far away from city lights, lie on your back for a long time and look up at the stars. If there is no light around you to diminish the brilliance of the firmament above, and if you stay there long enough and keep looking upward into that deep infinity, you will begin to feel yourself sinking upward into those stars. If you let yourself go, you'll slowly begin to become a part of that vast universe and the infinite eternity that beckons you.

When you finally lose yourself and everything of an earthly nature in the endless depths above you, it will not be your *brain* that feels the welcoming-home embrace of the stars. It will be your *mind*, your *will*, and the incredible limitless *spirit* that is you.

I Think, Therefore . . .

Imagine a world in which every single individual understood that everything we think can help create our lives in a healthier, more productive, more self-responsible way. Imagine the impact of even a single generation thinking that way! If you change the paradigm of how each of us, as individuals, sees our lives and the role we can play in the outcome of everything we choose to think, we will, in time, change the world.

If Descartes were with us today, knowing the neuroplastic brain as we now understand it, along with writing:

"I think, therefore I am,"

he might also have written:

"I think, therefore I can change."

Resources you can use:

Listen to Self-Talk Audio Sessions
from Dr. Shad Helmstetter
Stream Self-Talk programs on many subjects directly to your smartphone, tablet, or any listening device.
www.SelfTalkPlus.com

Life Coach Certification
(Information on life coach training and certification)
The Life Coach Institute
www.lifecoachinstitute.com

Certified Self-Talk Training
(Information on becoming a certified Self-Talk Trainer)
The Self-Talk Institute
www.selftalkinstitute.com

To Contact Dr. Shad Helmstetter
www.shadhelmstetter.com

Made in the USA
Monee, IL
09 October 2022

15511807R00164